THRIVER

My Story To Tell

What Domestic Violence Taught Me

And

How I Learned To Live

Doreen G. Lesane

© 2017 by Doreen G. Lesane

All rights reserved. In accordance with the U. S. Copyrights Act of 1976, the scanning, uploading, and electronic sharing of any part of this book without the permission of the publisher constitute unlawful piracy and theft of the author's intellectual property.

Thank you for your support of the author's rights.

Unless otherwise noted, Scripture quotations in this book are from The Holy Bible, new International Version Copyright ©1973, 1978, 1984, 2011 by Biblica, Inc,. ® Used by permission. All rights reserved worldwide.

If you would like to use material from the book (other than for review purposes), prior written permission must be obtained by contacting the Author at thrivermystorytotell@gmail.com

Exterior Photos by Ebony Brown
Covers Designed by Amelia Ladner

For information or to book an event for the author to speak live, please send request to thrivermystorytotell@gmail.com

Library of Congress Cataloging-in-Publication Data is available.

ISBN 978-0-692-95815-5
Manufactured & Printed in the United States of America

Author's Note:

I have learned to take nothing for granted, especially life, and so this book was not written lightly and may trigger some things for some people. It is not my desire to offend anyone.

This story is filled with *my truths*, my reality of what happened to me and it is told from the only perspective that I can tell it, mine as I travelled through the darkness and ugliness of abuse into the fresh air filled with sunshine.

I have learned not to be ashamed of my story.

What Domestic Violence Taught me and How I Learned to Live did not become evident until my process of healing began. I know that some will flinch at the idea that there are any lessons that can be taught from such a painfilled and painful place. Believe it or not, if you are breathing, you are not exempt from life and as such, there is always a lesson to be learned from what life throws at you. And from what it threw at me. Pain *is* a great teacher.

While writing this book, I struggled with how to write it and what to say in it. Ultimately, I felt compelled to be authentic about it all. It cannot be told any other way than how my life unfolded from abuse to abundance, from being a victim to being victorious, from being bitter to becoming better and from barely surviving to thriving. And yes, the stuff in between.

And in the midst of all that was wrong, I did not find God. He found me.

I did not hear His voice and for many years, I stayed as far away from the church as I possibly could. I am not going to say that I had an epiphany or heard this big booming voice and my life was instantly transformed. It did not happen like that.

It was a process that was taking shape the entire time that I was in the storm. The entire time that I was being abused. The entire time that I felt alone, He was there. In the storm. That is where and how my transition and transformation occurred. There is no way that I am still alive with my right mind, But for His grace and His mercy. And He is not through with me yet.

As I complete this book there is a shifting in every area of my life going on. I am still learning to Be Still and let God be God.

And as I continue to work with and advocate for those who have been broken by abuse, the similarities are uncanny and while our stories are unique to each person there is a common thread that shall forever bond us: What happened to each and every one of us……wasn't our fault.

It wasn't your fault.

It wasn't my fault.

The time has now come to share some of the untold parts of my journey.

The parts that I hope will liberate someone as I am.

The parts that I hope will encourage someone somewhere to fight for their life as I did and not to give up.

And the parts that were secrets yet no longer have the power to shame me into silence.

Please keep in mind that *this is not* a book of War Stories!

It is about darkness *and* sunshine.
It is about beauty *from* brokenness.
It is about myth busting.
It is about perseverance, of cleansing, encouragement and Hope.

It is a tale that resonates with all of us that has any type of exposure to or experience with abuse. It is the story that so many can relate to or identify with.

It is real, raw and radical.

And as you read this book, I hope that it changes your perspective of what a victim is *and is not* and that it provides clarity as to the whys of what they do, *of what I did*.

I hope that it inspires you to inspire others and that in one way or the other, you become a voice for someone suffering in silence.

The hope is that it changes your life.

It is my story to tell and in the pain, suffering and survival there was a refinement and a revival happening.

And I am better for it.

I hope that you will be better for it too and that it encourages you, to tell your story.

CONTENTS

Where Am I	1
Only Because I Have To	7
From My Brown Eyes	13
The Beholder	25
Apartment 3E	31
Doe Reen's Kids	39
Exactly Not Quite	49
Little Flower Lost	61
Knock, Knock	66
....About That Marriage	74
Horridays	83
If I were You...	90
Barriers	95
Summer 95	103
Preyed Upon	112
Imprisoned	116
Laundry Time	129
Forever and Two Days	138
An Intervention	144

By Default	147
For Now	155
Amen	162
It's About Time	169
Naked	175
Processing	180
Embracing Death	189
Stay The Course	196
Ready	204
In My Living Room	210
I Am Gwen....*Not*	216
A Matter of Opinion	226
A Drive By	233
The Flip Side	239
Who Knew	245
Such is Life	253
Thanks!	259
Thriver	262
Ms. Doreen	268

Photo courtesy of Gibney Dance Domestic Violence Awareness Month "I Am Against Violence "Photo Campaign October 2012

PROLOGUE

HEY BEAUTIFUL, THE TEXT READ, WHAT do you think about this?

It was a flyer for an Open Mic event and for some reason, it caught my eye.

Hey Auntie Sunshine, she texted back. Are you going?

Not sure. I know you write so I wanted to know your thoughts.

You should go Auntie.

Only if you go (lol)

Bet!

*****

We planned to go to this Open Mic out in Upper Manhattan at this Church and I spent the next two weeks trying to pen a piece.

No clue what I was doing. First Open Mic.

When the evening finally came, I started having second thoughts and my Baby Gurl had to convince me to go. We made there on time, but I was still having second thoughts and decided to just kind of watch and listen to everyone ahead of me before making a final decision of yes.

Suddenly it was my turn to go to the mic. I had to say a silent prayer because I wasn't quite sure how I was going to be received. After all, people were talking about love and work and art and children and politics and growing old. My spoken word seemed so, well, out of place. So I thought.

"Hi Everyone. I'm Doreen Lesane. I am glad to be here and well, umm, this is my first time at an Open Mic."

I put my glasses on and began:

"When I first heard about this, I knew that I

had to be a part of it

Cause everyday I'm in the heart of this

Domestic Violence

Too much silence

Children crying

Neighbors denying

Women dying

From the Silence

It's domestic violence

Another Task force, stars selling purple purses

No matter

Families destroyed, more bodies in hearses

From the silence, of domestic violence

Wearing purple, passing out ribbons

Why honor this human condition

Ignorance

Arrogance

Defeat

Death, yes, the Silence

All are products of Domestic Violence

But Hold on!

Wait a minute!

There's a simple solution

to end this pollution

Stop judging the victim

Stop embracing this crime

Take the time

to end the silence

Of domestic violence.

Simply.........

Speak up,

SPEAK up!

S P E A K U Pp!!!!!

As Sir Edmund Burke once eloquently put it:

"The only thing necessary for evil to triumph is for good men to do nothing"

Do something

S P E A K U P!!

Speak Up Against Domestic Violence.

speak up, I whispered.

It seemed like an eternity standing up there and the room was so quiet that if a butterfly passed through we would have heard the fluttering of its wings. In my mind, as I was kicking myself. something absolutely unexpectant happened.

One by one, the men and women in that room stood up and began clapping. I was embarrassed to say the least. Totally caught off guard by the response.

Then upon looking closer into the audience there were people who were crying. I went to sit back down but was stopped by the hostess. She thanked me for my piece and then disclosed to the audience that she too, had been a victim of domestic violence earlier in her life. Then another woman stood up and disclosed and another.

The show went on but afterwards several others wanted to speak to me and they too shared some of their story.

I left that place better than what I had entered it.

People were freed from their baggage and discovered that there is no need to be ashamed of their story, of where they had been.

But it wasn't always easy for me to be in front of the mic. That time was because I was allowed to share from a place of "go ahead."

Many times in the past, I was told what to say, which part of my story to tell, stick to the script they would say and I would walk away feeling used and abused and yes, controlled.

This night I felt humbled and privileged.

And light and emptied and free.

In a good way.

I felt that I was right where I needed to be.

It wasn't until the ride home that I began to tremble on the inside.

I started to feel claustrophobic and I was reminded of a day so long ago.

1

WHERE AM I

"*MISS, ARE YOU OKAY? ARE YOU okay?"* I kept hearing a man's voice asking if I was okay but just could not answer him. It seemed as if I let go of the grocery cart, I would fly across the store. It was spinning so fast that I didn't know what to do. After what seemed like an eternity of standing in this whirlwind, again I heard him asking me was I okay. This time I looked at him and said, *"Yes, just a little dizzy."*

What really happened is that I had a breakdown right there in the middle of that supermarket. I initially went to buy me something to eat and unconsciously filled the cart with enough food for a family of five. The problem is that there was no one home but me. It was the first time ever that I was alone. I had never lived by myself.

Ever.

I was the fifth of seven children. At fifteen, I was sent to live with one of my sisters who already had three children, then I had one of my own. Left her place, had two more, got married and had one last child. Then I got divorced but still had the four kids who eventually grew up and for the first time was home alone and it was not pretty.

I had no idea how to shop or cook for one person, *for me*. I had no idea how to take care of me. I was so busy taking care of everyone else. And for the first time, I was alone and forced to look at my life and all the things that had gone horribly wrong in it. I was clueless as to which flavor ice cream I like or if watching court shows were really as entertaining as I thought that they were.

I was lost.

My entire life up until that moment was not my life. *That Moment changed that.* That moment would set the course of my recovery from all of the abuse that I had suffered and endured. It would propel me into heights that I would never had known and it would create this new Doreen.

The one you know.

I spent the next fifteen or so years working on me and trying on life by going to the movies by myself and learning to spend time with me. I tried socializing a little at a time but would often retreat back into my world of pain especially when someone said something that I felt slighted me. I would attend functions if invited. But would still feel alone and many times, invisible, in the crowd.

I went to therapy and attempted self-help. I tried being a different kind of mother as well. But not just to my children.

I had to learn to trust again, to live without surviving. It was a really weird time for me as I experienced life from the outside looking in and trying to figure out how to get inside.

All of the things I was unable to do in that marriage then became some of the very things I would never do because certain things reminded me of him and those times. Others are things that I just choose not to do because they don't fit me.

There is another thing that I won't do.

No alcoholic beverages for me.

*****

He could be mean and violent when he didn't drink and much worse when he did. I remember one evening he was going to a function at one of his friends' house and took me along. He began to drink and when I was offered a drink I declined, and he became enraged.

"How dare you disrespect me in front of my people", he began whispering in my ear.

"You know I don't drink" I said while trying not to flinch.
"Tonight, you do.", he said.

So, I did.

And when we returned home I paid for disrespecting him and his friends home.

THRIVER: My Story To Tell

I was stripped and then the upper portion of my body was pushed out of the window six flights up and he told me that he could let me go, drop me from that window, and get away with it. Filled with fear, I tried not to look down or to panic. My torso was so far out that he could indeed let go and I would fall. I remained as motionless as possible hoping that he would pull me back inside. After he finished verbally abusing me, he raped me right there in that living room window. And there was nothing that I could do about it.

After all, every time the cops came, they left. And they left him there. He told them who his father was and they would leave. And he would continue to drink and continue to beat me. And continue to get away with it even when he didn't drink.

But in *that* moment, sitting in my living room by myself even that nightmarish memory didn't bother me. All that matter was moving forward, learning about me. Solitude became my friend and the need to explore how not to survive but to live became like a thirst that I could not quench.

Let me make one thing perfectly clear: When I was being abused, I never *just* a victim. I was *both* a victim and a survivor. Being abused made me a victim and surviving each physical attack made me a survivor at that moment.

Not a survivor when I escaped. But as the abuse was occurring.

And I was *not in* an abusive marriage. I was married to an abusive man.

Having to learn how to live, how to respond versus reacting, how to trust and how to just be me was not easy. I made plenty of errors along the way even trusting everyone that I came in contact with and getting burned, which drove me back into the shame, the pain and even self-blame. I needed to learn balance and I couldn't do it by myself, but during those initial years, I was all I had.

One of the most difficult things to move pass was my need to sit in the back of anywhere that I would go. It was really the only way I felt safe in the public. I needed to be by the exit so that I can escape if necessary. Facing the door worked well also. Even now, I am uncomfortable sitting in the front.

I admit, I was paranoid for a long time and if I encountered someone from my past, I would run into the nearest store, building, school, wherever I could hide and even behind cars. One day I even ran inside of a liquor store to hide. He was not going to find me. I would not go back into that specific side of town for any reason.

People don't get it and sometimes I believe don't want to. After fighting for your life against your abuser, family members and the systems created to help, it becomes tired some and for me, I just didn't want to hear crap from anyone. No ones' opinion about anything related to my babies or myself mattered.

My pain became anger and I lashed out at everyone. It was my way of protecting myself and my family because I learned that no one else would. I became *that* person, *that* parent, *that* patient, *that* client that no one wanted to deal with.

Sometimes it helped me to get what I needed done but more often than not, it hurt my cause.

What I have learned about that type of pain is this: it manifests itself as anger and it spills into every area of a person's life. It drives away people and opportunities become non-existent. And it hurts other people. My theory about that hurt people cliché is this:

>Hurt people hurt people...*unconsciously.*

It was never my intentions to hurt anyone. It was my intentions to prevent anyone from hurting me, but somewhere along the way I got my signals crossed.

When a person who is being abused goes into self-protect mode, hurting other innocent people is the last thing on their mind. It was for me. But when you are, *when I was,* in that much emotional pain, outside of my children, no one else mattered, and the truth of the matter is that when people know that you are a victim/ survivor of domestic violence, they will treat you like crap. They will. If you let them. Family, friends, co-workers, and even the system that is supposed to help you.

So yes, you do what you go to do to keep from being victimized by everyone including your abuser. Your signals get crossed and you end up hurting people *and hurting yourself.* I did what I had to do. I ended up hurting people. And myself.

That was not living and I was tired of surviving.

And then you find yourself one day trying to figure out, well, *I found myself* wondering,

Where Am I?

How did I get Here?

How can I get out of this?

2

ONLY BECAUSE I HAVE TO

IN ORDER TO GET A TRUE sense of how I ended up in such a life or death situation I have to take a trip back in time.

Only because I have to.

*****

My uncanny resemblance to my late father and always absent father who had a whole new family that he was raising caused me immeasurable suffering. As a child and well into my adulthood, I didn't understand why was everyone so upset and why was I being told that I was going to be 'no good like your father'. I mean, as a kid, you have no idea where that is coming from, what does it mean and why are you being told it. It also didn't occur to me back then that I would not ever be accepted by any of my siblings. Or my mother.

No matter what I did or didn't do and no matter how badly I wanted to be their sister.
Her daughter.

THRIVER: My Story To Tell

It just never happened.

So, this part of my story that I tell is just a formality to tie in how I believe that I ended up becoming ensnared in a life of abuse filled with betrayal and violence.

It is my solemn belief that being a victim of teen dating abuse and subsequently intimate partner violence and domestic violence was a direct consequence of my childhood, or lack thereof. While there are some moments that eventually became part of my healing process, for many years they were not.

*****

As the fifth of seven, there was no shortage of drama happening in that apartment. But it wasn't always like that.

Before we ended up at 1374 Boston Road, we lived across town at 1932 Crotona Parkway. It was through a series of unpleasant events that forced us out. You see, my mothers' oldest child had a habit. That habit followed him home and one day right after I returned from school there was a knock on the door. As soon as my mother opened the door, two guys pushed their way in and demanded money. It was all kind of crazy. When they left, they took me with them and told her that she better not follow them. She didn't.

At six years of age, I didn't quite understand what was going on, what just happened. I stood there in the hallway for what seemed like forever, not moving just as I was told by my brother friends who basically kidnapped me. Just stood there with the broom in my hand until a neighbor came into the building, saw me and took me back to the apartment.

That was the first of two push-ins. The second happened on a cold winter night after which my mother rounded us up and left that apartment.

The knock on the apartment door produced two guys that pushed their way in. One had a golf club in his hand and demanded money. There was none. One actually demanded that my mother take off her clothes which she did not. After knocking some things around with the golf club, they left and so did we.

The sound of the ice cracking under our feet on that cold December night as she took us down the street to a church where we stayed for a couple of days was my first experience with being homeless and would be the first of four times.

Subsequently we ended up living at 1374 Boston Road. That was the beginning of the end of the life I had known.

The first few years were relatively okay with the exception of going back and forth to the court. The cops caught one of the culprits and that was my first exposure to the criminal justice system. Every time we entered into that building, the former Bronx Criminal Court House, I would imagine that it was a castle. It made it easier to talk to all of those strange adults who kept asking me questions. The ceilings seemed like they were the height of a mountain and that spiral like staircase was just the most magnificent set of stairs that I have ever seen even until this day. Everything went downhill from there and my mother was never the same. I didn't understand why for many years, until I did. Childhood was never the same. It was filled with constant neglect, physical violence, hunger, molestation and all that comes with those things.

THRIVER: My Story To Tell

That court building still stands today in The Bronx, like an abandoned relic of yesteryear but even now, forty odd years later, in my mind I can still see that magnificent staircase. And I can still see Roy Prestons' face as he told me not to move...or else.

The resemblance to my father didn't make things easy for me. *The siblings* mistreated me just as my mother did plus the fact that they were angry that he was with the kids he had from the other woman.

My only place of comfort and safety was school. My favorite subject of all time was a reading class where the teacher taught Current Events. You know, the Five W's; *Who, What, Where, Why* and *When. And,* the best place in the world was the school library. It was such a magical place. I loved books then and I love them even more now. My love for books helped me to escape from the realities of the horror that I was living in and at home my time was mostly spent sitting in a corner reading a book that I had gotten from school. Before things spiraled completely out of control, I was very fortunate enough to get a year subscription of *Readers' Digest* one year for Christmas.

In fourth grade, there was this one book that I read and was totally mesmerized by, *"One Hundred Dresses"* by Eleanor Estes and Louis Slobodkin. The main character in the book is a little girl named Wanda Petronski. Our home and school situation were very similar. But she was bold and stood up for herself in spite of her situation. I wished that I was strong like her. I know that she is just a character in a book, but my nine-year old self could really identify with her and I aspired to be like her. I liked her and of course the dresses. I still have the book over thirty years later.

Once I got to middle school nowhere was safe. Being from a house filled with utter chaos placed me on the side of the Have Nots and the bullying and teasing was constant whether it was at school, home or in the neighborhood. Getting good grades didn't help at all because I then became a target for those who wanted me to give them the answers and would harass me afterwards if I didn't. School then took on a somber tone and I started to flunk my tests on purpose to get them to leave me alone. My only hope of escaping the nightmare was reading.

But I had to be careful! My mother was religious. Books were banned. Music was forbidden. We were not allowed to play with other children when we went to the park and she *never* spared the rod. She would take (drag) us from the Bronx to a variety of churches in Brooklyn on Friday and Saturdays nights. We were not allowed to do anything that didn't line up with her beliefs. Nothing. Period.

And then there was Saturday. The Sabbath. The Lord's Day. There was no movement. Not even cooking. Beef bologna and cheese and Seven up. Every Saturday. Week in. Week out. Month in. Month out. Year in. Year out.

We were taught to turn the other cheek (as quoted from the Bible) and as a result defending ourselves ended up being pretty much left up to how each person, well defended themselves and if caught fighting, *there were consequences.* I didn't know how to fight. Not physically or verbally. I was too afraid to fight, plus, because of my no-win situation I knew better than to even try. I was also taught that children are to be seen and not heard and that what I had to say was not relevant. I thought that I would go to hell if I disobey or questioned what she said that the Bible said. Because she said so.

Explanations were never given but a *"Because I said so"* always was.

I also didn't know what to think. My only focus was trying to prove to my mother that I wasn't going to be 'no good' like my father (whatever that was) and that I was worthy of her love. It was a huge responsibility and in my quest to do so, I became a semi perfectionist and a people pleaser and that was a burden. Both choices made by a kid who had no idea just how damaging both were.

It would take me well into adulthood before I was able to get a firm grasp on several things: One, *that all of that was a lie. All of it.* Two, that nothing that happened was my fault. I just happened to be present. And three, it was just preparation. Harsh lessons but in the end, well worth it.

My introverted personality and love for reading combined with my fear of my mother and siblings, helped me to adapted to being alone. It didn't stop the beatings, emotional abuse or the other stuff that was happening. It did make it easier as crazy as that may sound.

At fifteen, I was instructed to go stay with my older sister to help her out with her kids for the winter. When the winter was over, I was told by my mother that I couldn't come back home.

For the next three years, I stayed at my sisters' home in less than ideal conditions.

It was during that time that I was introduced to teen dating violence at the hands of my first two children's father and how family members of abusers contribute to and enables the abuser.

3

FROM MY BROWN EYES

REALITY IS NOT ABOUT YOU UNLESS it is *your* reality that you are speaking of. Perspective on anything is based on a persons' personal experience in life to any given situation and that is their reality and cannot be discounted or refuted.

A persons' reality is like pain. It is like fear and it is like love. All three are subjective to the person that is experiencing it. Whether it is Fear. Pain. Love.

It is their reality.

Not yours. It was my reality.

The Fear and the Pain.

There was no Love.

The years of verbal, emotional, psychological, sexual and physical violence at the hands of two different men, at two different periods of my life and during my childhood was my reality and will always be a part of who I have become.

THRIVER: My Story To Tell

One person cannot truly feel the depth of another's pain and emotion and shame and confusion. Not even if you have experienced a similar situation.
You can imagine. You can empathize.
You can compare your war story to theirs.
You may be able to identify with another.
But you *can never* truly feel or experience the same, *exact* pain or emotions as another.
My reality is mine and is subjective to my experience as a former victim.
Domestic Violence, or in this case Intimate Partner Violence, when viewed from the victim perspective is really what it is about.
Viewing it and voicing it from *my* experience is not about discounting any studies, research, terminology used or any of that.

It is how I view domestic violence as it relates to my experience, what I experienced, endured, and escaped from.
It, *my experience*, had nothing to do with all the fancy terms like ripple effect, honeymoon phase, walking on eggshells or safety planning. The stone that was tossed causing the ripples does not adequately describe how the abuse occurs and continues. There was no still stone sitting down on the bed of a river, the ripples did not subside, the ambience associated with a honeymoon was replaced with sheer horror and brutal physical and sexual abuse and I walked on shards of glass instead of eggshells.
And safety planning?
In my world of intimate partner violence, surviving was really Safety planning.

The only plan I had was not to die.

Safety planning victim style looks much different than safety planning that an organization do for their clients. You call it Safety Planning or Seeking Safety.
Victims of abuse calls it Surviving The Best That They Can. And Staying alive.

Exactly like when I was a child.

Domestic Violence may be common, but it is not normal or ordinary. It is Extreme and Extraordinary and you do, *I did*, what I had to do to stay alive. To live to see another day. To see my children another day. Survival has a way of making people do things that they would not ordinarily do. Going along to get along is another way to stay safe. You don't make any waves. You don't contradict anything thing said or any order given. You can do all of those things and still find yourself abused.
But you are still alive. I was still breathing but not really alive.
Learned helplessness? I am still trying to process *how*?
How in the world did this phrase become relevant to a person being abused?
Why would anyone want to learn how to be helpless?
I didn't learn *how* to be helpless, I, as many others were, *was forced into a state of helplessness* first from being abused, then from seeking help and not finding any.
It is easy for those outside of the abuse to judge the abused person and take on an air of superiority by shifting the responsibility of the abuse that is occurring on the victim.
This is not about finger pointing or blame. It is about the reality of what abused women (people) endure

and the victim blaming statements that are ascribed to them by society. Learned helplessness. Really?

*****

There are no metaphorical expressions to describe the reality of the terror and the experience that a person who is being abused endures. Not for me anyway.
Not from my perspective as one who survived.
But if I *had t*o describe my pain during that time, it would be like water that someone had poured into a box which slowly destroyed the box then flowed out spilling everywhere. More like water that had come to a full boil, scalding everyone and everything that it came in contact with it.
Some days I was the water but most days the box after the water was poured into it. There were days that I was in so much pain, I couldn't contain my emotions or myself.
My pain was more of a rage and for years after I healed from the pain, I was embarrassed at how many people I had unconsciously hurt. *And then I wasn't.*
One of the hardest thing to do is to get people to understand where you're coming from as it relates to domestic violence, or intimate partner violence as it is interchangeably referred to. That is what empathy is about.

No abused person wants pity or sympathy.

You see, operating from a place of trauma robbed me of the freedom to enjoy life. It stole my sense of safety and emptied me of trust. It wasn't living but more like existing and to a very large degree, feeling invisible.

PTSD my former therapist said. Post-Traumatic Stress Disorder was the official diagnosis.

Always on edge and always feeling like something was about to happen. *Always ready to run.*

The fancy word is hypervigilance and it is a symptom of posttraumatic stress disorder.

I will not sugar coat the truth about domestic violence because it is real. What happened to me was real.

Just as real as you are touching this book and reading it.

I could *feel it*, the blows and the fingers strangling me just enough to cut off my air supply, to let me know….

I could *taste it*, the blood, so much blood in my mouth and at times flowing out of the corners that I would almost choked on it. *And I know what it tastes like to have a loaded gun jammed in my mouth.*

I could *see it,* the look in his face as he stared into my eyes while raping me. Or when he lectured me on *how I made him beat me.*

I could *smell it*, the odor of my own death on his hands as he beat me unconscious or stomped on my body after flinging it into the wall. On several occasions.

I could *hear it*, the sound of my own voice unrecognizable from the screams and the screams of my babies, for help falling on deaf ears.

And I could *touch it,* when I picked up the clumps of hair that he ripped from my scalp or the speed knots that were sitting very prominently on my forehead or the stitches that held the wounds together.

Every bit of it was real.

The nightmares and the insomnia.

I was in many ways, paralyzed.

It wasn't a dream.

It wasn't perceived as the people say and the fear was far from false.

I mean what is fear from the perspective of a woman that is being abused? From the perspective of anyone caught in the vicious cycle of domestic violence?

Fear is defined in the Merriam Webster Dictionary as (noun) *an unpleasant often strong emotion caused by anticipation or awareness of danger.* It also states that fear *is reason for alarm.*
I was married to a man who choked me, beat me, stomped me, raped me, intimidated me, threatened to kill me, attempted to kill me, stalked me, deceived me and yet to the outside world, my Fear was False.

The Expectation of a beating or a beatdown was not False.
The Appearance of the bruises and clumps of hair pulled from my scalp was not False
Being dragged by the hair from one side of the street with traffic coming at you to the other side wasn't an imaginary event nor was being push down a flight of stairs

after having my daughters' birthday cake smashed against my face.

The Reality of all of the abuse that I endured, *that I experienced* was not False.

The acronym for FEAR is not False Expectations Appearing Real….. Well, maybe to you but *never* to a person being abused.

Not ever.

Fear is *real* and it is in the eye of the Beholder.

Fear is far from false and the feeling of experiencing it never quite goes away.

The Fear that strangled me and entangled me and rendered me helpless and hopeless was real.

Like Domestic Violence, it was cruel.

It was a living nightmare.

It was terrifying.

It was everywhere I looked or went.

Including in the cemeteries.

Men, women and children who have been murdered by abusive partners and parents and misunderstood by society. I am quite sure that they all feared for their life.

And as I feared for my life, I too, also ended up in the cemetery.

*****

*"D*oody, ba ba ba Doody, you love me?*"*, he kind of sang the cats' name and the cat wagged his tail in a big circle.

"You love Tay?", he asked the cat and again Diamond wagged his tail in a circle and we all started laughing.

My son proceeded to ask the cat if he loved each of his other two sisters and each time the cat would wag his tail in a circle, almost like a fan. But before he could ask him if he loved anyone else, my former spouse got up from the couch and walked over to the cat.

"Hey Diamond, do you love me?", he asked. The cat did not move or look at him. He asked the cat again if he loved him and before we knew what happened, his size ten and a half feet was on Diamond's neck and he was making squishing motions and cursing the cat. The cat was trapped under his feet and screaming. The kids started screaming. I didn't move (*I knew better*) but asked him to please take his foot of the cats' neck. He lifted his foot of the cat, who ran for his dear life, told the kids to shut up and go in their rooms and then he calmly walked over to me and lifted me by my neck from where I was sitting. He then pushed me up against the wall and began to strangle me for making him look bad in front of the kids.

That's what he said.

I only asked him to stop stepping on the cats' neck.

The look in his face was of pure rage. That was the first time that he had choked me to this degree and I couldn't breathe.

    I.
        Couldn't.
                Breathe.

I struggled somewhat trying to free myself but knew better than to touch his hands to get them off of my neck.

And as I gasped for air and slowly began to slip into unconsciousness, he let me go. I fell to the floor and he began to stomp me. When he finished, he walked out of the apartment door and left me lying there.

Because I asked him to take his foot off of the cat neck.

That was my reality at that moment and believe me when I tell you, having the imprints of his hands on my neck coupled with not being able to swallow solid food for almost two weeks or being able to do simple housework was not a mirage. I was not imagining the pain. Or the beating. Or the *fear* that ensued.

What many don't realize and I didn't know is that most abusers do not strangle to kill but to control. The act itself shows that they can so it is important to realize that when a person is strangled, she is on the edge of homicide.

I was on the edge of a homicide. *My own.*

He would put both hands around my neck and began to squeeze it.

First very slowly and then with more intensity.

He was showing me who was in control and just how easy it would be to strangle me to death.

Only he didn't strangle me to death.

Just unconscious.

Just enough to prove his point.

My survival of strangulation by my former spouse only emboldened him to do it again and at one point became part of the norm.

It was used to establish and reaffirm his position of power.

It is also used as a weapon to control the abused partner.

It worked flawlessly.

That and the opened hand slap. A swift and unexpected blow to the side of the head was not uncommon, and actually was quite the norm that it should not have been.

Between the beatings and the choking, he was in control.

The sad part is that I knew that I could have been murdered at any time.

A *real* victim of intimate partner violence, the true victims are dead.

Murdered by their partners *and* the silence from society.

*****

It was and now all of these years later, I am free from him and not the consequences of what he did.

Strangulation, like many of the other physical acts of abuse causes long term health issues and which may not manifest themselves for many years.

In my case, it wasn't until eight years after I was free from him that my hearing started acting up. I awoke one day to the fact that the hearing loss that I now experience was in the same ear which the eardrum had been perforated so many years ago from an unexpected punch to the side of the head. And the headaches have become more frequent.

The impact of the beatings eventually takes a toll on the body. The health industry has no idea just how many patients walking into medical environments are being abused and never report it out of fear of being judged. The number of women *that never* receive medical attention is staggering. I meet them all of the time and understand their reluctance to go into a medical facility.

I too felt that same reluctance.

I wish someone would have even pretended to care about how I sustained the injuries that they were stitching up or providing pain medication for or taking x-rays of.

I wish that as the doctor drew that diagram of my back on his notes to indicate where the bruises were, that he would have asked me how did they get there.

I wish that the day I had to get my wrist stitched up, that someone would have asked how did your wrist get cut. As I write this and think about how damn mad I was at myself that day for feeling like a coward, that I punched my hand straight through the mirror because I should have done something. *Anything* after he had beat then raped me for saying 'not now'.

THRIVER: My Story To Tell

I wish that the day that I walked into the clinic with all of those purple and green fingerprints around my swollen throat, *that just one person* in that establishment would have asked if I was okay.

I don't wish for myself but for those who are currently being abused and visiting health professionals who just brush through the questions... not really even waiting for an answer.

4

THE BEHOLDER

IT IS NOT EASY TO EXPLAIN what it feels like to be abused then blamed for the abuse.
It is not easy to explain the feelings associated with that abuse.
It is even harder to explain that when you leave my presence, I resent you because you get to leave.
I didn't.
You think that when the police knocked on my door and was having a conversation about how they hate coming to the same apartment over and over again, that I liked being in this situation.
How do I trust you when you have already judged me before I have even opened my door?
And you? Why would you cuss me out because your kids couldn't sleep last night *because* I was being beaten but you won't dial 911 *because* I am being beaten.

Can you see things from my perspective?

For one minute, don't be the officer responding to that call, don't be the neighbor who sits in a huddle with the rest of them, don't be my sister, brother telling me that I am stupid for staying.

Don't be that sister in church ignoring me or worse, gossiping about me. Your prayers make you feel better, not me.

Try to be me…..just for a moment.

I am not asking you to walk a mile in my shoes.

I am asking you to just put my shoes on, you don't have to even walk in them, just put them on, then *if you can*, judge me…or just *imagine what it may be like in my shoes.*

Until then, don't personalize my attitude toward you.

I am doing the best that I can in this moment, you know being a victim of a crime that society calls domestic violence. Or this act of social injustice.

I am not myself and don't know who I am from day to day due to my situation.

My nasty attitude, or my resistant behavior toward any assistance that you may offer is my way of protecting me.

I know that you think that I am stupid and confrontational.

I know that you don't get it.

Is it because you don't want to?

THRIVER: My Story To Tell

Is it easier for you not to care?

I can tell you that I care, that I am really a nice person, but I can't show it or convince you because you just see what's on the outside of me. Including the bruises.

Not my insides where I am afraid and just need for someone, somewhere to care just enough for me to trust, Because I don't trust anyone. Not even myself.

I don't know if I am coming or going.

My options were limited to who my abuser was and until I feel safe again, I can't trust anyone.

You see, you and everyone else sees me from the outside of the circle.

You are looking in and from that posture, you cannot get what has *really* been going on with this thing called domestic violence.

You cannot fully grasp the horrors of my life and that everything I do or say is based on staying safe the only way that I know how.

Like that time, he was beating me in the street and that man intervened and I flipped out on him. While everyone present thought that I wanted him to beat me like a dog in the street for all to see, that is far from the truth. It was my way of thanking you for stopping the beating. If I had stood there and done or said nothing, the beating would have continued. I had to protect him to show him that I cared. That I loved him.

Even though I didn't. I don't.

In reality, what I was doing was staying alive and staving off another beatdown.

I know that you don't get it, but in that moment, I was using my skill of Safety Planning.

I was in Survival Mode. I was afraid. And tired.

Taking his side prevented another beating.

For that day anyway.

I know.

You still don't get it.

And you won't unless you have been abused.

Unless you have personally been in my situation, you will never get it.

I can use some assistance, some guidance, maybe some resources to point me in the direction I am trying to go.

I don't need to be controlled,

Where to go, what to do, how to do it, how to say it. What time to be there.

That was my abusers job.

Is it yours too?

THRIVER: My Story To Tell

I will always appear to be resistant, confrontational and just plain nasty and rude to you, to others.

To those who are seeing me as a Victim, disempowered, helpless and voiceless.

How do I smile, laugh, trust, live when my life was in such turmoil? In danger!

As the Beholder, I tell you that I couldn't.

And I couldn't get stronger because I keep getting judged by you and those like you who don't, can't or won't take a look through my eyes.

I couldn't get stronger because I had to fight you and those like you to prove that I am no longer a victim.

You will always judge me and others like me.

No matter how far removed I am from that situation, you will always refer to me as a Victim.

You will always think that I am helpless, but I am not.

I will always have to fight to prove you wrong.

You will always place me on the Survivors Panel.

Even though I have done more than that.

Become more than that.

Close your eyes and just imagine.......that your life *was just like mine.*

Or your loved one is the One who is being abused.

Would it make a difference then?

5

APARTMENT 3E

THE YOUNG ADULT WOMEN THAT I had the privilege of providing the Teen Dating Awareness group to at a prominent agency for youths confided in me about the nightmares of living in those homes and how even removed from the situation, some by force and others by choice, the nightmares continue to invade their dreams. Initial contact with them was, well, as expected. Rough.

"*Miss you ain't one of us!*"

"*Whatcha know about being beat up?*", she demanded to know,

"*Look at you all fly and speaking all proper. Please!! How you gonna tell me something.*"

"*Get outta my face with that.*", the other young lady said.
"*I don't wanna hear about no domestic violence.*"

THRIVER: My Story To Tell

"Excuse me Miss, but I ain't trying to hear what you got to say.", said the one that I pegged for the voice of the group.

"You come up in here like we want to hear about some domestic violence stuff. Ain't nobody beating me."

They were loud and rude and ready to fight.
Their very behavior screamed I don't want to hear this because I lived this and I am still in pain.
Not my first time working with this age group. The initial behavior is always the same.
I reached into my bag and pulled out THE picture of my face battered with my finger in a sling and gave it the loudest one and for a moment she looked shocked.
She was speechless.
I turned back around and continued to set up for the session.
As the other girls gathered around her looking and gasping in horror, I heard her say,

"Is that you Miss?"

"No, I said *That used to be me but I don't want it to be you."*
They were ready.
I then told them that the person standing in front of them didn't always look this way or talk this way.
(That experience taught me to never dress like that for this age group again.)
That I wasn't always fly, more like busted from head to toe and a little crazy.
And according to everyone who knew me back when, I wasn't nice. At all.

They all looked shell shocked like they didn't know what to say and the one who invited me to go home now sat quietly.

As the workshop on Teen Dating Violence made its way through the allotted time, the young ladies present began to ask questions which I answered honestly and without hesitation.
One by one they told their stories of living at home and the abuse of their mothers. Some told of how the step father/ father/boyfriend would try to manipulate them to side with him, even telling them that the mother deserved what she got. Still another spoke of how the mothers' boyfriend tried to come on to her when her mother was asleep. Then the one who was the loudest, now the quietest, raised her hand and said, *"Miss, this happened to me before I got here."*
I smile and nodded as she continued to share her story with her peers.
And as one of them told her story, I heard one of my daughters' voice, the young lady sitting before me was telling my daughters' story and how she ended up not liking her mother very much because her mother would allow the boyfriend back after he had beaten her in the public.
It gave me chills and made me more determine to pursue educating and advocating others about what domestic violence really is.
Not what the text books says. But what it looks like to the victims/survivors.
Funny thing about this (not ha ha funny) is that as I was standing before that group of young girls discussing Teen Dating Violence, they had no idea that from the ages

sixteen through twenty I was being abused by my two older children father before they were even born.

They had no idea that I sat in the same lounge that they were sitting in when I was eighteen with my then nine-month old son.

They had no idea that I too was once a resident at Covenant House.

*****

The last two years staying at my sisters' place was pure hell for many reasons. Including the fact that I was being physically abused by the guy in Apartment 3E. I guess we were boyfriend and girlfriend. We hung out a lot and even used to go to the movies and baseball games at Yankee stadium.

That all changed. His mother didn't like high yella girls and referred to me as uppity and even called me a house negro (she actually used the other n word). I don't recall how or when it became abusive, I was dealing with not wanting to be where I was but had nowhere to go. So, when it happened it happened.

It started subtly. A pinch here or there. A rude comment then straight dissing me in front of his friends. Then one day he came upstairs to get me and once I was inside his place, he beat me up and locked me in the apartment until it was time for his mother to return home from work.

Locked you in the apartment??

Yes. Locked me inside. His mother had the double lock on her door. The type that when locked from the outside if you didn't have a key to unlock it from the inside, you could not get out. I would either sit in his room until he came to let me out or sleep all day until he came back. This happened many times until his mother made it home before him one day.

THRIVER: My Story To Tell

I was seventeen being abused and also being held hostage by my boyfriend.
He was cruel and mean. I remember coming out of the building one day and as I started down the block he called me over. I kept walking. He called me again and when I did not respond, he caught up with me and ripped my sundress off of me. It was a nice crisp white one with these beautiful pink flowers and green leaves. I really liked that dress. Only got to wear it that one time. When I started to struggle to break free from his grasp, he slammed me into a car and began to punch me in my face. I had to go to the emergency room at Bronx Lebanon Hospital up on the Concourse. Well actually, he walked me to the hospital then walked me back home. I was unable to see out of my left eye for almost two weeks. My sister never asked what happened to my face. Neither did his mother but his grandmother did. She was the only voice of reason back then but was really unable to help me.
Later that summer, he physically assaulted me again in the street. He had a handful of coins and when he struck me, a dime became lodged in the side of my temple and I had to go back to Bronx Lebanon Hospital Emergency Department. Once again, took me and waited while the doctors extracted the dime out of my right temple, stitched me up and sent me about my business. Even now, some days I still trace the now barely visible scar with my finger in disbelief that my body has withstand such physical violence.
The physical and sexual assaults continued after I became pregnant. He became much more violent and while his mother still hated me, she found me to be a source of extra cash and used me until he almost killed the baby in my stomach by brutally assaulting me then flinging me belly first, into her kitchen wall when I was seven months

pregnant. I was sent back upstairs to a life that really wasn't any better. There was no physical violence, but the conditions were unbearable.

Up until I became pregnant, I was attending A. Philip Randolph Campus High School. We were the inaugural class and was housed on the campus of City College. It was an interesting time for me. It was really the first time I had ventured out of the Bronx and while home was a continuation of crazy, I really liked high school…and I felt safe there.

At about five months pregnant, I was discharged from there. Back then all of the pregnant girls were sent to the Martha Neilson School for Pregnant Girls. It was on the third floor of Junior High School 136 on Jennings Street in the Bronx. I was in the twelfth grade with three months left to graduation when I gave birth and with no one to keep my son for those final three months, I dropped out of school to care for him.

When my son turned eight months old, I was done with staying at my sisters' and done with my sons' father and his mother. One day, I walked in from the hospital with my son, placed his birth certificate and immunization card with three pampers in a bag. I then went to my sisters' room and told her that she was free to toss everything I left in the garbage. I walked out of her apartment and never looked back. I had about twenty dollars to my name and no clue where I was going so I went to the local police precinct and told them that I had nowhere to go. After speaking with me for about a half of an hour, I was given a piece of paper with an address written on it.

That is how I became a teen mom resident at Covenant House. I would go on to homeless for the next three years living in a homeless shelter in Mariners Harbor, Staten Island called the Conco De Oro Motel.

Life did not get any better. There I made a series of wrong choices including informing my sons' father where I was. Two of those years was spent having the crap beaten out of me and having another child, a daughter from him. During this time, he had also taken my son and fled. Thank God I was able to get him back. Those three years are a book by itself.

I later became involved with another man whom I had a daughter with four years later.

*****

I really didn't notice when they first entered the train. I just looked up and there they were. A young mother, her child in the stroller and the guy sitting next to her. They were having what appeared to be a civil conversation, but one thing changed that landscape.

He sat there relaxed, smiling and touching the baby's hand while the young mother sat there pregnant, tensed and just kind of staring ahead with her right eye swollen and discolored on the outside and bloodied on the inside. On the same side of her face, her lip was swollen and bruised with the skin broken. Freshly bruised.

I felt angry that she looked like that.

I felt angry that each and every person on that side of the train car saw that young lady sitting there, bruised and battered.

And I was angry that there was nothing that I could do, knowing that if I said anything, that it would more than likely cause her a beatdown.

I also began to feel like I was suffocating and started to sweat profusely. Seeing her sitting there reminded me of my own experience as a teen mom being beaten. Seeing her brought back so many emotions. So many memories of what that man and his mother did to me. It was a horrific time for me. There was zero contact between him and I once our daughter turned eighteen. I made sure of that.

But in that moment sitting across from her, my stuff from a time long ago was triggered and I was overcome with emotions. As soon as the train pulled up into the station and the doors opened, I rushed out gasping for air.

It wasn't even my stop.

6

DOE REEN'S KIDS

MY MOTHER NEVER LOST HER SOUTHERN accent when she came to New York from South Carolina and always called me Doe Reen and my children became Doe Reen Kids. One son, three daughters. I won't be telling their full story for they are all adults now and I have to respect their healing process and where they are. I will, however, have to share some as my story would not be authentic and true without them.

They lived through the horror and experienced it just as well as I did. My reality included them and my desire to stay alive was more because of them than my own life. The thought of what would happen to them if I die kept me alive. Period.

My son was always smart and talented. He could write and read like it was nobody's business and by the time he was in third grade was reading newspapers front the front to the back. Very mild and easy going. He was born when I was eighteen. Outside of having severe asthma and being hospitalized for it several times before turning one, he was in good health. Great sense of humor and all of these years later when I see birds, I always remember how frustrated he would become because he couldn't catch them no matter how fast he ran.

His personality changed dramatically over the years starting with him becoming aggressive towards my oldest daughter. I already had the first three when I met my now ex-husband and so he was present when my sons' behavior started to change. I had no clue that he was even aware of what was going on with the abuse and no clue how bad would become.

It started so subtle then escalated to full blown violence and my son learned how to cook and clean and care for his sisters because I was too battered. What I remember the most about this time and my son is how, as little as he was, how he tried to protect me from this grown monster who had no mercy on me and no regards for them.

"Help!"

"He's killing my mother! Help" he would cry as he ran down the length of the sixth floor, banging on the doors.

"Somebody please help us".

No one would open their door and more often than not, no one called the police. To really give you an idea of the extent of neighbors "minding their own business", the woman that lived next directly next door, was dating a cop. A New York City Police officer. They never opened their door either.

My son attended cadets on the Saturday faithfully for years and was great at being a cadet. He was honored on numerous occasions and absolutely loved going. So much so, that on Friday nights he would spit shine his shoes and iron his uniform so perfectly that you would have thought he was already an enlisted officer. He loved roller blading and hockey and was taking Tai Kwon Do. But at the end of the day, not knowing if I would be dead or alive when he returned home, robbed him of what he enjoyed doing and eventually he stopped enjoying them

My son grew up to not respect anyone in authority. He had to fight to walk down the street he lived on since he was three years old. He was bullied and tormented and teased as the boy who father beat his mother. He was also physically attacked. He was beyond angry.

The worse part of this is that the same people whose door he would bang on for help turned into the same people who wouldn't let their sons play with him. He was ostracized and isolated and labeled as bad kid. That was so far from the truth. There are no bad kids.

His third-grade teacher once told me that each morning when he got to school, that he would just stand and look out of the window. She said that one morning she asked him to sit down and he said that he had to stand and watch and when asked why, she said that he said that he wasn't sure if his mother would be alive when he got home from school. That was reported to me during parent teacher conference and I just did not know what to say.

Like his sisters, he was haunted for many years by the memories of that neighborhood and like me, never returned once we left. Until I had to.

My older daughter, brilliant and reading proficiently by second grade was on the other hand, not having it. When they teased her, she struck back. She became a fighter and would fight any body any age anytime. She dealt with the trauma from all of that the best that she could. She was always out going and popular. She had style and knew who she was before she understood the concept. I call her my Big Girl.

With my two oldest kids, things were even more complicated. Although I was no longer with their father, I did allow them to visit his mother. I thought it was the right thing to do. However, since she never really liked me that was no easy feat and caused me many sleepless nights and even a night in Central Booking.

My middle daughter, whom I call Mija was like a magnet. Everyone loved her. Everyone was drawn to her carefree personality and that smile that was always on her face. And she used to sing like a songbird. And she danced like no one was looking and oh could she dance! Her years in grade school were filled with school plays, solos on the children choir and being friends with just everyone. She appeared oblivious to all that was happening. But as things changed, she changed.

My youngest daughter, whom I call Baby Gurl is very introverted yet artistically inclined. Like my son, my daughters also suffered with asthma. By the time my Baby Gurl was three years of age, she knew when an attack was coming and would go and get her nebulizer for a treatment. Academically, she was smart as a whistle like her siblings and in the fourth grade made the District Superintendent List. She had scored a perfect Four on both the Math and Reading State test.

She spent many years suffering from severe depression and used to self-mutilate. She said it eased the pain she got from the memories playing in her head of when her father would beat me as he held her in one arm. She began to eat to feel better.

My daughters, sang in the children choir, played basketball and were cheerleaders. Both my first and middle daughter enjoyed performing in school plays but as the violence at home continued, their involvement decreased.

None of that was enough.

For eight years of their lives they were unfortunately exposed to the abuse. They experienced a life that no child should have to. They grew older watching their mother being beaten, spit upon and flung into furniture. The black eyes, busted lip, broken nose, broken jaw, finger prints on the neck, speed knots and broken furniture that were part of their everyday existence throughout the years were not easily erased with the calm days....the ill termed honeymoon period that came every now and then.

They experienced others outside of the household remaining silent, judging them, harassing them and forbidding their peers to play with them. They grew up having to fight just to be outside in the summer air.

And they grew up emotionally distressed, in pain and very, very angry.

The hurtful and derogatory words that my ex-husband spewed at me was now their everyday vocabulary. They cursed at me, threatened to fight me and yes, were also physically violent toward me.

But in spite of it all, they were my babies.

I don't tell this to disparage them or shame them but to show how the horror that they lived became a part of them.

They didn't ask to live in that environment and while I thought nothing of how it would affect them long term, *the reality is as a battered parent you can't and don't think about those things.*

When you are being strangled and it feels like that persons' hands are beginning to go through the bones of the neck, the last thing on your mind is ten years in the future.

When a parent is being abused, any children living in that home is also being abused and that stays with them long after the violence is over. Helping a parent that is being abused is more than crisis intervention, it is about long-term assistance. For the family.

It didn't matter how nice the furnishings were or that there were presents under the tree at Christmas. It did not matter that they got to go away to camp during the summer or if they were fortunate enough to indulge in extra-curricular activities. If there is violence in the home, those things do not make up for the atmosphere.

It didn't for mine.

It didn't matter to the many women that I am contact with who are now mothers and grandmothers and still vividly remember their fathers beating their mother.

It is in understanding what happened to me and how it impacted them that they have begun to pick up the pieces of their scattered and tormented childhood and move into their young adulthood, knowing that there are better days ahead.

In spite of it all, I needed for them to know that I always loved them no matter what and that I understood that some of the things that they had done were a direct result of what had happened to *us*.

Yes. Us. It happened to all of us and not just me.

Society still don't get it. They don't want to.

I have heard others say that it is just an excuse and to them I say shame on you for trying to hold a child accountable for the actions of criminal acts that they witnessed perpetrated on their mother.

Shame on you.

Many children end up being physically and/or sexually abused just as the mother is being abused.

My son was physically abused by my abuser. One of my daughters was psychologically manipulated to believe that I didn't love her and how could I prove him wrong when I was in no position to protect myself or them.

My children experienced the same trauma and post trauma that the I did.

These children, including my own grew up with what society calls being dysfunctional.

My children weren't dysfunctional. They were victims who survived domestic violence. I often call them the littlest victims.

As I was being abused physically, emotionally and psychologically, my children were also being emotionally and psychologically abused. Their little minds too fragile to comprehend the nightly screams of *"Stop! Please Stop! You're hurting me"*, the pleas for help for which they couldn't help and no one else did.

I don't even want to imagine what was going through their minds hearing me crying *"Please stop. Get off of me. You're hurting me. Please stop"*

Their young impressionable minds confused by the body sized dents in the living room walls and blood, well, over everything. Broken furniture and the place in total disarray. Their eyes blurred then becoming accustomed to the black and blue marks over my body, the bruises in my face and at times, my inability to even talk from being choked or to get out of the bed from being beaten.

They adjusted to the point where they stopped crying when he was beating me and most times would just go get in their beds until I stop screaming. They had become desensitized to the yelling and screaming.

But Not Really.

Yes, the battle was real and the war zone was my body, the furniture and walls and even the cat.

*****

All of the things that research say about the effects on children who are witnessing or have domestic violence are true. The trauma that follows them forever is also real and based on their personal experiences.

It followed mine. For a very long time.

It is much like the fear that the person being abused experiences.

You don't feel fear, you *experience* it.

A person *experiences* intimate partner violence.

Trauma is the same and when a person who has not experience childhood trauma tells a person who has, "to get over it" or that "it was a long time ago, you should be over it" or "that it is not that serious" has no idea what they are talking about.
In fact, what they are doing is re victimizing and re traumatizing that person by negating their feelings and minimizing what has happened to that person.
Many adults who come from households where there is violence as children are presently doing the best that they can. Their presentation may be rough and their attitude may be tough, but for them, without therapy (and sometimes in the midst of therapy), they are operating from a place of pain. They are doing the BEST that they can.
Mine grew up to do the best that they could.

During the course of rebuilding our lives, my children were not just regular teenagers. They were teenagers with trauma.

As I grew stronger and wiser, I realized that I had to apologize to them for what they experienced. It wasn't fair to them and they did not deserve to have to live like that.

One by one, at different junctures in their lives, I apologized. I told each of them that I was sorry that they had to be in the midst of all of that. I explained to them that I did the best that I could during that time. I told them that I understood why they were so angry at life and *at me* and that they had every right to feel what they did. I told them that I was sorry and I asked each one of them to forgive me.

I apologized to them as a family and individually, I asked to be forgiven. I had to apologize for them living in that apartment.

The truth of the matter is that even this very day as I sit and write this, it is still a process for them and there is one that has not forgiven me.

Maybe One day. I continue to pray.

We are still working things out all these years later.

We have good days.

We have very not so good days.

Or weeks.

Sometimes Months.

*****

My children, as with all children are not witnesses to a family dispute, they are victims of the crime of domestic violence.

There, I said it out loud.

My children were victims of domestic violence.

When a mother is in that level of abuse, it is all that she can do to stay alive and survive through the next attack and the next attack.

When I was in that level of abuse.

It was all that I could do to stay alive.

For my kids.

There is always all of this talk about how the abuser isolates the victim.

Yet everyone else does the same thing when they shun, shame, blame, refuse to let the children play together, when they judge and ridicule the abused parent in front of and within earshot of the child(ren) and all of the other non-supportive and judgmental things that they do.

News Flash: *Society isolates the victims as well.*

All of the time.

And me?

After a while, I preferred it that way.

7

NOT QUITE RIGHT

FROM BEING SEVERELY ABUSED TO ENGAGING with hundreds of victims/survivors over the past nine years, I can tell you that they, *that I,* have an issue with some of the descriptions used to describe domestic violence.

*****

As a professional, it is the jargon, the lingo, used in the field but those of us who have experienced and endured domestic violence, know that some of it is just not the right way of describing it and is misleading.

To me anyway.

We really are the experts on what domestic violence *is and is not.* Experience trumps education. Always.

I am an Expert on the subject of Domestic Violence. Not only because I studied it. Because I lived it.

I experienced it, endured it, survived it.

Escaped it.

Yes, I do have bone to pick as someone who survived physical, emotional, sexual, psychological, spiritual, financial abuse at several different periods of my life. The jargon used is not quite accurate.

What my personal experience with intimate partner violence taught me is that what I learned formally is not quite in line with how victims actually *experience abuse*. Let's take a look at the top three of those terms. First, the Honeymoon Phase, then Ripple Effect and Learned Helplessness.

The Honeymoon Phase, this term is used by professionals as a way of describing the Cycle of Abuse. It is when the physical violence has *temporarily* stopped and things *appears* to be well within the relationship.

Domestic violence is a not a relationship issue. It is a crime with one person deliberately controlling, being abusive, manipulative, threatening and assaultive to the partner and not one person that I have ever met or assisted *ever* described that calm period as being on a honeymoon or like a honeymoon.

I didn't as a victim.

I don't as a professional.

It is often during this time that the abuser may feel pressure from the law or is just straight up plotting his/her next move through seducing the victim into a false sense of security that they have changed or that they are willing to change.

This is when the abuser presents himself/herself as being apologetic, willing to get help or even willing to help as a partner should in a relationship.

This is often the calm before the storm as described in the technical description of the Cycle of Abuse.

There is absolutely nothing loving and respectful about this time frame as most victims are just as fearful as when the abuse is happening.
I was.
This is not a time of reflection for the couple to be thinking back to when they first met and all was right with the world.

This time is for the abuser to continue his/her carefully crafted manipulation in a way that dupes the victim to believe that things can go back to how there were in the beginning *or* that things will improve.

This term is deceiving in that it portrays the absolute opposite of what this time of abuse is about.

And for young adults, it almost romanticizes and even to an extent normalizes the abuse.

All relationships have ups and downs. True. However, not all have abuse. I used to struggle to understand *where* is the romance in all of that. At what point does the honeymoon with the private suite, champagne, hugs and kisses and mutual love and respect show up in a relationship where one person is completely dominating the other through various forms of manipulation and physical violence. Just because there is no obvious or physical abuse happening at that moment does not make it romantic. I mean, it was difficult to stay focus sitting in a support group for abused women with the facilitator talking about a "honeymoon phase".

The abused person is still being abused emotionally mentally and psychologically which is why there is a cyclical effect happening.

It is not a honeymoon.
It is war.
It was war and I didn't want to be a casualty.

When things were good, they were well, okay. There were no arguments or disagreements. There was no verbal or physical violence, but for me, there was always the thought that there could be. Nothing romantic about the thoughts of being physically assaulted the week before and now the person is rubbing your thighs wanting sex. That very moment can turn into a beatdown if I rejected the advances.

What do you do? *What did I do?*

To keep the peace, I let my abuser have sex with my body as I tried not to give any indication about the disgust that I was feeling, how each time his lips touched mine, it took all my strength not to vomit.

It is called Survival Sex.

And for me, Marital Rape.

You see, victims of domestic violence have no choices contrary to popular belief.

My only choice was to let him have his way or get beat down. I learned to avoid beatings this way and spent quite a few nights silently screaming while he raped me in his choice of position.

Many nights were also spent waking up to him on top of me. In me. Was it marital relations or marital rape?

Either I flowed with it or I got the beatdown.

Which would you have chosen?

But there were other times, I chose the beatings because the sexual assaults were just as vicious. Like the time he beat me up then placed a pillow case over my head, raped me then got up in the morning like everything was right in the world and the world calls this the honeymoon phase.

And as for me, I never walked around on eggshells. It was more like shards of glass.

THRIVER: My Story To Tell

As I sit and listen to so many other women recall their stories about how terrifying this time period is, there are times that once I return to the quietness of home, I find myself thinking back and remembering that because you don't know what is really going on his mind during this time, it really makes those moments scarier because you don't know if he really meant what he was saying…..about being able to kill you and get away with it.

Will tonight be the night that I die?

My kids, what's going to happen to my kids if he kills me?

Those are the thoughts that ran through my mind each time he choked me or beat me in my face.
Those are also the thoughts that ran through my mind during the "honeymoon phase."
At least you know what his thoughts are when there is the violence.
Not so much in the silence. For me, there was always that thought that it might be the *one* punch that kills me. Nothing romantic about that.

*****

The Ripple Effect is another term that when analyzed by someone who has been victimized by their intimate partner makes no sense. *When analyzed by me through my personal experience.* Once again, as I sat in that support group, and listen to her speak, it just made no sense as she tried to describe domestic violence.
This seemingly apt description of domestic violence is so deceiving. It states that domestic violence is

akin to "the ripple effects from a stone being thrown into a body of water and the water cascading back to the shore." In essence, the surface of the water is disturbed by the stone and it causes ripples of water to form moving out toward the bank…now I had to repeat that to create the visual which makes no sense. There is a problem with that description. *For me.*

From the perspective of me, a person who was brutally abused for an extensive period of my life.

The stone representing abuse and the disturbance of the water is the "the impact of domestic violence" and the ripples of water supposedly is how it flows into other areas of the victim life, his/her community and ultimately society.

Now, *if that theory was true than once the ripples subside, domestic violence would be no more,* however, that is so far from the truth.

The fact of the matter is that domestic violence is more like a living and breathing entity that has permeated every area of society. It has taken on a life unlike any other crime and a fair description of it would be more like a fungus or an octopus, where the abuse is the head, the body is the person being abused and the tentacles are the various areas that are connected to that body,

Let's use the theory of the Ripple Effect and compared it to the Octopus as all things relate to the domestic violence. Once the stone is thrown into a body of water, it is inactive and sinks to the bottom of the river bed. It doesn't move from where it has landed, and it *cannot* move again unless it is moved by someone or something. On the surface of the water, the ripples move outward in rings toward the shore and eventually those ripples subside and the water becomes tranquil unless a disturbance occurs. For example, another stone is thrown into the water *or* another act of abuse or violence is committed.

On the other hand, the octopus is alive and its tentacles flailing and ever moving as long as it is alive…*as long as the abuse is occurring*.

As long as the head and body are attached and as long as the octopus is alive, there is movement and like domestic violence, there is movement, hence the abuse. As a victim of domestic violence, there was no rock lying on the river bed. The abuse and physical violence was alive with every area of my life being impacted. Home, family, work, neighbors, and I became who I was: An abused person, a victim/survivor of domestic violence.

As a wife, mother, sister, daughter, student, customer, even as a stranger in the street. Every area of my life had become infected and affected and there was no way out. When I first heard about the Ripple Effect and how the waves ultimately subside all I could think to my self was, No.

That is not how it happens.

For me, there were no ripples but waves from the thrown rock that kept growing in intensity and kept crashing against the river banks. As a child and as an adult.

Even then as I sat back and thought about it, this isn't how family violence or domestic violence works.

There is nothing stagnant about it.

It is fluid and keeps moving.

It doesn't just stop. It travels and infiltrates.

It takes on a life of its own and there is no one size fit all solution and the consequences of it are wide and deep. It is about life *and death*.

The real victims are the ones that were murdered.

The effects of domestic violence are ever moving and far reaching.

All of the Best Practices has not and cannot combat or eradicated it.

Nor will it. Because it is tolerated and by some celebrated.

The reality of the abuse for the person experiencing it is not the reality for society.

It will *always* be under reported for many reasons including the fact that the victim *is always* judged, blamed and shamed.

The resources available are not enough. Especially safe, permanent and affordable housing. The laws are not enforced.

Best practices work on paper and may work for some victims but never all and *never* the majority.

There are no one size fit all remedies and each victims' circumstances are unique to who their abuser is.

Best practices do not work because it is black and white and domestic violence isn't.

There is nothing black and white about it.

It is multi colored and multi-faceted and victim/survivors are faced with multi barriers.

It is red then black and blue and yes, even purple.

Not like the ribbons.

But never black and white, *never* cut and dry.

It is challenging and convoluted and even confuses and confounds the most respected professionals in the field. There is nothing professional about domestic violence unless you are speaking of an abuser who goes from women to women (or man to man) abusing them, thus making being abusive his/her profession.

It is the worst best kept secret. It is the secret that kills.

THRIVER: My Story To Tell

Everyone knows about it and everyone knows someone who is being abused *or* who the abuser is.

Turn on the news and you often find that when a story runs about a woman being murdered by her husband, ex-husband, boyfriend or father of her children, there will be that person who says, *"Oh yeah, they fought all of the time."* Or *"There was always screaming coming from that apartment."*

The neighbors know.

The people down the block knows. Even the children who don't live in that apartment knows about the lady on the block who is being beaten.

Everyone knows.

*****

There are a total of one hundred eight- five apartments split between four building where the bulk of the abuse against me took place.
Everyone knew.
And once he became bold enough to beat me in the street, everyone watched. Even the neighbor kids.
That particular day I refused to go with him to his parents' house. I just did not want to go. He had already spent the past two days verbally abusing me, assaulting me with his words. His words were harsh, demeaning and sliced deep into my very soul.
Verbal abuse stays a lot longer than the bruises and broken bones that come from the physical abuse. Words are so powerful. They give life and they bring death. Abusers wield them as weapons that attack the controlled

partners identity and self-worth thereby eroding a person's value of their self. They are used to intimidate, create self doubt and insecurities. The words are used to isolate and are emotionally and psychologically abusive. Verbal abuse is a manipulative tactic that has long term consequences and for many victims, the harsh and derogatory words become triggers that create a life on edge even for those that escape and long into the future.

It did for me and for so many that I now work with who are still trying to heal from the verbal abuse.

(Whoever said, *"Sticks and stones can break your bones, but words will never hurt you"*, you lied.).

Didn't matter, that day I wasn't going. He even tried to manipulate my oldest daughter by telling her that I loved my son more than her. I said nothing. I didn't want to get beat up. He told me to get dressed again. After I said I wasn't going the second time, he punched me in the face, knocking me to the floor then he grabbed me by my hair and dragged me out of the apartment, down the stairs, out of the building then up the four stairs and across the street with on-coming traffic.

I had only a tee shirt and sweats on. No shoes and the entire time, he held me by my hair so that I could not get to my feet to run and when he got me across the street, he slammed me up against the car so he can get his keys out. Once he opened the door, I began to struggle with him in hopes that he would lose his grip on me. It only made him angrier.

As he opened the door and try to push me into the passenger seat, I struggled to break free. He punched me in the mouth and knocked out a tooth.

THRIVER: My Story To Tell

The blood began to flow from my mouth and as he pushed me onto the sidewalk, he started calling me all types of profanities, jumped in the car and sped off. When I composed myself enough to get off the ground, (no, I did not bother to look for the tooth) I turned to cross back to the other side of the street and there were about ten people just standing outside of the building. They had watched the entire incident. They stood there smoking their cigarettes and with their children and no one intervened.

No one said anything.

No one called the police.

Everyone *saw* and everyone *knew*.

As usual, I made my way back into my apartment to do what I usually did. Try to be as normal as possible.

The crazier thing with this episode is that his mother called and asked why didn't I come over and when I told her, she blamed me for the whole thing and said that I should have just done what he told me to do. I told her he had punched me in my face and dragged me out of my apartment and across the street with oncoming traffic. I told her that he knocked my tooth out and she called me a liar.

Yet, it is still whispered about and society is still uncomfortable hearing about it.

This is the silence that can kill and often do.

Ironically, if he had murdered me at any point and it became a news story, the neighbors would have gone on camera as saying, "Oh yeah. He beat her all of the time, everybody knew."

8

LITTLE FLOWER LOST

The church had grown dark and suddenly I couldn't breathe. As I ran towards the front to get out, the tears began to fall and I had to hold my mouth to keep the cries from escaping. *This was really happening.* She was really dead inside that urn her sister had purchased for her ashes. Her body was beaten beyond recognition and instead of letting the machine acted as her lungs, they made the decision to let her go.

Most of the work I have found myself doing is because I wasn't murdered. She was. She did not deserve to die like that and her son, my god son and my children godbrother did not deserve to lose her like that.

Intimate partner violence kills and the cemeteries continues to be filled with innocent women.

It is only by the grace of God that I lived.

*****

Diane was beautiful like a flower. Her disposition was just as exquisite and her soul was like the baby breath that stood out among the bunch of perfectly wrapped flowers.

She wore her hair pulled back into a ponytail with a long extension down her back and was always smiling and tossing her hair. My son and her son clicked the first day they met and were friends until her death. My son was seven and he was six. She didn't have any girls and over time my daughters became her daughters and she even renamed them. Granny, DaaDaa and Bud. I kept telling her that they would never answer but I was so wrong. They answered her every single time and they loved her and they loved their god brother.

They loved that flower that she always wore in her hair behind her right ear and they loved going downstairs to her apartment. She taught them the fine art of eating crab legs and how to have fun while doing so. In her own way, she spoiled them rotten and I let her. They loved their God Mommy and she treasured them.

She was married to the guy on the first floor and at first, he treated her nice. Then slowly that changed. He began to berate her while they were outside. When I would visit her apartment, he tried pretending that he was cool but after a while was just who he was but never disrespected me. After all, he knew who I was married to and everyone in the building just kind of didn't bother me.

Although that changed after he started beating me in public.

We were both being abused by our husbands and as weird as it sounds, at that time we just lived with it and went on with our daily lives. Our stories were so similar yet so different, but we were connected through our children and neither one of us identified with being abused. We never talked about our situation. We never acknowledge the bruises or black eyes or the busted lips that one or the other had at any given moment. We just went about our lives the best that we could and so did our children.

Once they moved up to the fifth-floor things for her really got bad.

Reflecting back on that time, I can recall that even then I noticed the physical changes in her. She stopped wearing the ponytail after he slapped her in the lobby and pulled it off her head that day. He stepped on her flower and pushed her in the elevator saying all types of nasty things to her. He said she had no business outside with her friends when he wasn't home. She began to lose weight and her clothes no longer fitted her. She began to drink and drink and drink but my children and I still loved her. She was still our flower. She was sweet to everyone and to all the children in the building.

She still laughed but it began sounding hollow and only happened when he wasn't around.

I recall arguing with someone one day because they called her a drunk and that is why he was beating her. We all knew that was not the truth. When she moved into Five Seventy-Five she wasn't drinking and walking around with tape on her glasses. She wasn't floating in her clothes with her hair barely combed.

Our friendship lasted until her death and our children grew up together and when it was time to get mine baptized, there she was. The incident that led up to her death produced nightmares for me for many years and there were times when I felt so guilty. *Why didn't I go upstairs to check on her that day?*

Because I couldn't.

Two nights before she was beaten to death, I was also beaten. On the day I found out, I was leaving the building to go up the street to the doctor to get my back looked at and hopefully some pain meds. Her spouse was standing on the first floor and as I was walking passed him to exit the building, he said, *"You should go check on your girl."*
I looked at him and said, *"F*** you"*, and proceeded to walk out of the building.
When I returned about two hours later, another neighbor was standing in the lobby crying. As I started to walk by her she grabbed my arm and simply said, *"Diane is dead."*
I don't remember crying or how I got back to my apartment. The next few days was a blur and I don't remember telling my babies. I know I did.

I just don't remember when.

Her body was cremated the day after she was taken off the ventilator and I arranged for a memorial at the church we were attending at the time. The day after her memorial, her sister came to my apartment and gave me Diane's coat. It was a black mink fur with a patch of red fox on the sleeve. I have had it well over twenty-three years and I have not ever worn that coat.

Every now and then when I think of her, I will put it on and just sit on my couch and think about our lost little flower and how her life was taken from her and how she was taken from her son and from my children. The one thing about her death that have never left my mind is how that could have easily been me. I could have died in that same building and in that same manner.

Why her and not me? I often asked myself.

He was never charged with her death. For a long time, I stopped speaking to him. After I forgave my ex-spouse for what he had done to me, I forgave that man as well. Being angry at him served no purpose and would never bring Diane back. It would never ease the pain that her son or my children had to live with. I heard that he has since passed away time and we have never seen her son again.

All of these years later, I still miss her and her death made me take a look at my life.

It is her death that compels me to do more than just survive but to live life and to help others find their way back to life from domestic violence.

*****

These stark realities about intimate partner violence are frightening. The deafening silence of the many who witness victims being abused and say nothing.

The normalization by society and the murders of not just the victims, but their entire family.

Everyone connected to the victim becomes a victim.

9

KNOCK, KNOCK

I USED TO WONDER HOW DID my babies always end up in Mary's apartment and it wasn't until maybe five years ago when one of my daughters and I were talking about something totally unrelated that the question came up.

About two months after the lady who was dating the cop moved out, Mary moved next door with her four children, three sons and one daughter. One of her sons was a rough little kid and he would always be banging on the wall. It drove me crazy and I really wasn't in the mood for it.

Had my own problems.

One day the kid started playing around and bumping into the wall. I opened my door and rang her doorbell multiple times and when she opened the door, let's just say my choice of words were not neighborly.

Actually, I was just not in the mood, you see, the night before, he came in drunk and it was an all-nighter. I had to sit up and listen to him rant and rave about how his car was acting up and he didn't have the money to fix it and how he wasn't drunk but I probably thought that he was and just one of those nights that turned into him fallen asleep on the couch and me sitting there until sunrise, knowing that I dare not fall asleep before him and I dare not disturb him.

After being extremely rude and un neighborly, I returned back to my apartment. The next couple of hours were spent listening to my new neighbor yelling at her son to sit down and that irked me as well. All I wanted was peace and quiet. The kids were in their rooms and I didn't know where he was at nor did I care. I just needed to be ready for if he decided to come over.

Quite honestly that is how I lived back then. I mean that is how I existed.

Always on edge and trying to be ready.

Just in case....

*****

One night after an incident (I don't know what else to call the beatings), I couldn't find my babies, not one of them. My son always ran out of the apartment screaming for help and this night, I thought that the girls had gone out behind him. I ran to one of the exits and they were not there, so I began screaming their names. Within two minutes they came running up to me out from Mary's apartment. As she stared at my bruised face and torn shirt, she didn't say a word. Neither did I. Just gathered up my babies, walked into my apartment and closed the door.

The next morning someone rang the doorbell and when I opened it, there stood Mary and her children. She simply said, *"I'll take them to school for you."*

I told her to mind her own damn business and closed my door.

Hurt people hurt people....unconsciously.

It was never my intentions of being rude, disrespectful or un neighborly. I had grown accustomed to no one helping or caring. The norm was for everyone to pretend like they did not hear me screaming for my life. The norm was for no one to open their door as my son ran up and down the sixth floor banging on the doors screaming,

" *Help me!*

" *He is killing my mother!!"*

"Help Me!!"

Not

One

Door

Would

Open.

Not One.

So when Mary came along and opened her door, it was shocking to say the least and totally unexpected.

By then I was not a nice person.

I was broken. Lost. Hopeless. Angry.

I was fed up with how the neighbors judged me but never helped me.

Don't know why she's knocking on my door.

Nosey.

This scene must have repeated itself for about a month, including the beatings until one evening the doorbell rang and there stood Mary with a pot of Arroz y Gandules con Carne.

"This is for the kids."

She stood there with the pot stretched out in my direction.

This particular day, I just couldn't.

I. Just. Couldn't.

The night before was long and brutal.

That was the night he showed me his gun and the bullets in it and that was the night he put it in my mouth (of course I did, opened my mouth just as he instructed me to and *so would have you*) and told me that he would kill me or I could do as he said. I did exactly what he told me to do and how he told me to do it and my kids almost didn't make it to school.

She didn't say anything else. Handed me the pot of food and went back into her apartment.

I fed my babies and it was at that moment that I realized that I couldn't help myself or my babies and it was the most helpless, humiliating and haunting moment of my life.

And Mary, sweet Mary, never judged me.

She never said a word about the screams that she heard from the other side of her wall.

She never complained about my body being slammed on the wall that separated our units.
(And I had the nerves to be complaining about her small son playing up against the wall)

She never once suggested that I leave.

She never noticed the black eyes or busted lips or the big bumps that adorned my forehead.

She never said a word to my then husband whenever she saw us together. He would say hello to her and she would not say a word and eventually he stopped speaking to her.

There were some other things Mary never did.

She never stopped bringing food over for the kids.

She never stopped her sons from playing with my son.
She never stopped taking them to school even when I was well enough to.

For four years, this woman, practically a stranger, never stopped caring and many years down the road what she did for us, saved my son life one night.

It was about fifteen years after all this, that my oldest daughter told me about how they always ended up in her apartment. We were having a conversation about someone that lived in that neighborhood that my daughter had ran into earlier in the week. Then we started talking about Mary.

I asked, *how did ya'll always end up at Mary's house* and she said," *She told us that when he started to fight you, to listen for the knock on the wall. My door will be open for you all."*

A simple knock on the wall.

I started to cry and couldn't stop.

How rude and nasty I had been to her yet, she only saw my situation and not who I was in those moments.

She cared for my children without any questions and no judgements.

She never asked for a dime.

She never threw it up in my face.

She did not have to do anything for my babies or me.

But she did. Unconditionally.

In that moment and even now, there were and will not ever be any way to ever thank her for that small gesture of compassion for my babies. There are just no words to express the magnitude of gratefulness that I have for what she did so many years ago and as I often share that part of my story at trainings, I always tear up. Even now as I share with you, my readers, my heart swell with a debt to this woman that I can only repay by showing others the same compassion that she showed to my children and myself.

The memories of her gift, her kindness and compassion during that time extended seven years into the future. We had already escape from our abuser and my divorce was final.

*****

One night my son came into the apartment. He had gotten into an argument with someone and was going to go back outside to fight. I pleaded with him and tried to block him from leaving and as we stood there, him telling me to move out of his way and me telling him that was ever happened outside let it stay outside.

"Please don't go back out there.", I said, *"It's not worth it."*

"Move Mommy!! You don't get it. If I don't fight him, there is always going to be a problem with him."

"I love you. Please don't go back downstairs."

"You don't love me!

"You don't care!!

"Nobody cares about me and nobody cares about you!!", he shouted.

"When he was beating you, nobody helped us and nobody cared!", he shouted and was now starting to shake. As I stood there between him and the door, I realized that my son was still holding on to the pain of all those years

past. He was having a nervous breakdown right before my eyes and for the life of me, when I opened my mouth to respond all I heard myself say was, *"But Mary cared."*

Immediately he stopped.

He stopped shouting.

Seriously. He stopped.

He stopped crying. He just stopped and stared at me. Time seem to stop as well as the situation went from one thousand to zero at the mere mention of Mary's name.

His entire demeanor shifted and he looked at me and said, *"I'm not going back outside because of Mary."* He went into his room, came back out, looked at me then took a shower and went to bed.

That night I witnessed the power of just one person caring. One person cared and the power of that one person had long term rewards for a young man who needed it in that moment. I saw and I learned how what is said and done could have far reaching rewards or conversely, consequences.

Ten years after Mary moved into that building, although we were no longer there, the sound from her knock on the wall and her very name was still a sound of safety for my babies. The mere mention of her name created a sense of safety, a safe space.

10

NOW....ABOUT THAT MARRIAGE

IN FULL DISCLOSURE I DID NOT know that person well enough to marry him. I absolutely cannot change the past so there are no "in hindsight" or "if I could change what happened". I cannot and so there are no regrets. I won't say that I was wrong or that it was a mistake.

*****

I knew that man less than two years and he asked me to marry him three times before I did.

And that union fell really short of a marriage.

The wedding was small and happened on a humid and rainy day in May. It was pouring rain and lighting and thundering and there was no honeymoon.

From the very beginning, it was wrought with abuse, lies, infidelity and interference. I don't believe he ever loved me or even knew what love was or is. I don't he was capable of loving himself. At that time, I had no clue that before me, there were others that he had abused and fathered children with and that while he was with me, he was also abusing a woman in another part of the city and fathering children with her. That means that one of his sons was born the same year that our daughter was born. She is four months older than him and they both were about four or five years of age when I found out.

Most people probably would say that I had low self-esteem but the truth is whether I did or did not, *it didn't give him the right to batterer me.*

It doesn't give anyone the right to abuse their partner.

I will speak more to the low self-esteem theory, as I call it, later in the book. What I will say about it right now is that it is victim blaming and makes the victim accountable for the actions of the abuser.

I did not marry him because I had low self-esteem or felt worthless or had nothing better to do. I married him because I believed that he was who he said that he was, and I trusted that he was sincere with what he claimed that he felt for me. I never ignored the warning signs,

I didn't know them.

It can be difficult to spot an abusive person since they are very crafty with selecting their victim. Their overall demeanor is often unassuming when they first approach their prey. More often than not, the psychological abuse is a way of conditioning their victim prior to the physical abuse. That doesn't hold true for each case because each case is unique to who the abuser is. This is often the case whether it is a woman or a man being victimized. Many are empowered by the people in their circle who know that they are abusive and says nothing.

I had no clue that I was being abused or what domestic violence was. Actually, back then *all I knew* was abuse although I didn't understand that it was wrong. That was my norm and with no one to tell or show me different, how was I to know different.

I know *now* that my prior history of abuse during my childhood played a huge part in me marrying that person, however, it still doesn't justify the abuse.

I fully believe that growing up and being abused as a child led to me being abused as a teen/young adult and subsequently becoming a battered wife. Coming from a place of abuse during my childhood made it easy to go with the flow. I had been conditioned to be quiet, that no one wanted to hear what I had to say, that I would be no good like my father, that the husband was in charge, that I needed to stop being smart and after suffering from extreme verbal abuse, for me it was just normal to be spoken down to. After all my voice had been stolen a long time ago.

I now believe that my initial instinct to not marry him was correct and I believe that marrying him was the only choice I knew how to make given my background.

Blame the victim. Judge the women, the abused who stay, for whatever reason.

It is an easy out for those who don't care, don't want to care, believes that it isn't their business, or want to remain on the sidelines.

It's not my business they say.

It is not my place others say.

THRIVER: My Story To Tell

I say to those who don't care, believes that it's none of their business or between husband and wife, *please,* step out of the way of those that do care and want to make a difference for people that are experiencing abuse.

Please and Thank you.

And the judgmental folks who have these preconceived notions that the victim is well aware that she is being abused, when in many cases victims of domestic violence do not self-identify. Practically zero self-identify. Like many that are being abused, you really honestly have no idea what is going on. In other words, they do not consider themselves as victims.

I didn't for many years.

I had no idea what the hell was going on until a professor tried to explain to me that the bruises I was coming to class with were signs of me being abused.
Domestic Violence he called it.
The irony is that I sustained the injuries to my face on that occasion *because* I was in school.
I was studying for my Associate in Computer Science while obtaining my GED through college credits. Eight years had passed since dropping out of high school to care for my son and the time was right to return to school.
Anyway, I had just returned into the neighborhood one day and I ran into one of his friends who was like," *Hey Gwen, congratulations on that Masters".*
"*Hey T, what are you talking about,* I asked.
"*Your old man told me that you're in school to get your Masters."*

Without thinking I said, *"Oh no, I'm studying for my Associates. Computers."*

We talked a little more and went our ways. Later that evening he came over and was actually acting like all was well. After about an hour he asked to speak with me privately in the bedroom.

Once the door closed behind me, he slapped me so hard that blood flew out of my ear. He commenced to beating the living daylights out of me. I never saw it coming and as I sit here right now writing this, that was one beatdown where I never cried. I was too shocked by the attack. I was being punished for correcting his version of what degree I was studying for.

It was an honest mistake.

One that I was careful to not make again.

I got up the next morning, made breakfast for my children and went about my day. Including school. It was there on that Tuesday morning that I first heard the term domestic violence. And even then, I didn't grasp the concept.

Until thirteen years later.

Honestly. I did not understand what it meant *to be* a victim of domestic violence or to have my place deemed a domestic violence household.

Yet, it is exactly what I was.

Another preconceived notion, is that she must like being beat, so she stays. Unless you are a batterer, you know that makes no sense whatsoever. I did not like being beaten, raped, intimidated, terrified, stalked.

I did not.

That marriage wasn't a marriage. It was more like a hostage situation for me.

And he had all the power and control.

Through force and through fear.

Power and control is truly the best way to describe what Intimate Partner violence is. It is NOT about love or anger. There is nothing pretty or sweet or entertaining about. It is not just a social justice issue. It is a crime.

*****

A woman attending a training I facilitated on domestic violence made a very observant point: Sometimes an abuser will beat their partner one time and that one time is severe enough to establish who is in control and what could happen if the partner doesn't comply. She was/is absolutely right.

There is no one size fit all on how to abuse your partner. Or how to spot an abuser. Some are so crafty that you can never tell that they are abusive until you are invested in them emotionally.

Being in a marriage that contains abuse on any level is just a non-existent way for the person being abused to live. Realistically, you are not living.

I wasn't. I was surviving….barely. But I wasn't living.

My own contact with law enforcement came during a time when being married meant that what happened in that marriage was a "personal and private issue between a man and his wife" and in my specific case, his father was politically connected, held a high position wearing that white shirt to work each day and belonged to a lodge. He always made it a point to remind me who his father was and when the police did show up, he would tell them who his father was and they would just leave me there.

   Bruised, Beaten and bloodied. *Just leave me, us there.*
Like the night he broke my sons' arm while I was downstairs at the laundry in the building. All of those factors came into play how he was able to do what he wanted to and absolutely get away with it.

  As I was finishing the laundry, he came down and said, *"Your son stole ten dollars from my sister and you need to have a conversation with him."*
(That has never been verified).
I didn't say anything but ran out of the laundry and up six flights to my apartment to find my son crying and holding his left arm. His arm didn't look right and we were going to the hospital. I gathered up everyone, dropped the girls off to my neighbor and ran outside with my son.
As far as I knew, he never came upstairs and when I got back downstairs, I didn't see him. I flagged a taxi, pushed my son inside and as I went to close the door, he pushed his way into the taxi and shut the door. I started screaming at him to get out. Before I knew what hit me, he punched me in the side of my head and as I raised my arms to shield my face, he let off a barrage of punches into my face.
  The taxi continued to drove toward the hospital with the driver screaming. *"No! No! Stop that! Get Out! Get Out!"* but he continued to punch me and by this time we arrived, there was blood streaming from my nose and mouth and the entire time, my son sat there frozen. With

nowhere to run. Stuck inside of that taxi as I was being brutally assaulted.

Blood was everywhere.

When the taxi pulled up in front of Lincoln Hospital, the driver started yelling for us to get out. We did and as I tried to grab my son and run into the emergency room, he snatched me up by my neck and threw me up against the gate. That is where I was, up on the gate with his hands around my neck and blood still streaming from my nose and mouth when the squad car pulled up. My body was pressed against that fence with blood and obvious injuries to my face. My son was just standing there holding his arm and splattered with my blood. He held up his hand with his wedding band on it. He said his father's name. They got back into the car and they left. He relaxed his hand around my throat after he said it was my fault that he beat me up. He pulled me off of the fence pushed me to the ground and he left. Left us right there and when we entered the ED, no one ever asked me what happened to my face. My son was triaged and as we waited for his arm to be x rayed, his mother showed up. Out of nowhere.
    She didn't say much to me but spoke with a nurse or doctor and in less than an hour, the x ray was done, his arm casted and we were done. She dropped us off at home and that was that. The incident was never spoken about and his family went about life as if it never happened.
    But it did.
    That was *the* moment that I realized that I was in real trouble and that no one would help me. Or my children.
    Every now and again, one of my children will bring it up. And it becomes a long conversation filled with tears.

About what if he had really killed me, he would have gotten away with it just like he said that he could.

I will say that I wasn't supposed to die and as cruel or weird as it may sound, it was all part of the plan for where I am now.

Yeah, *about that marriage.*

*****

Many years later, my son and I talked about this and other things that had taken place. As a teenager, he was done and bitter about it all. He could not understand why no one would help us, why I just couldn't take them and run away.

Later on in his late twenties, he called me one evening and told me that he understood why I couldn't get away from that man and that he was no longer angry at me. He said that he knows that he need some therapy to get away from the memories, but that he wasn't ready.

He stated that he realized that I had done the best that I could under the situation that we were in.

And he told me that he loved me.

11

HORRIDAYS

It is crazy how the holidays were so horrifying. Just days filled with sheer horror in overflow. There is just something about the holidays that victims seem to be terrorized at such an alarming rate. These were indeed the most horrific times of the abuse.

Birthdays, Easter, Labor Day, Memorial Day, Fourth of July, Christmas, *if it* was a holiday then it was guaranteed that something was going to happen.

So much so that many years later, long after we escaped and the marriage was over, we, my children and I opted not to celebrate any holidays.

The memories of the horror was still very fresh and ingrained in our minds.

What I remembered the most is how people just pretended like all was well. His family, the people that we were friends with individually and collectively, the neighbors and even strangers. Hanging at the picnic all bruised and battered. The people there eating and laughing and having a great time.

Then there was me. *Me.*

The elephant at the picnic instead of in the living room. Being avoided and being ignored. I mean, what do they say? How do you have a conversation with the person wearing the finger prints around her neck or who can't enjoy the food because her mouth is all busted and bruised? *What do you say? What can you say?*

*****

I remember, one year his father had come over a couple of days before Christmas and after giving the children their gifts, he gave me a small wrapped box. I said thank you and placed it under the tree. He told me to get it and open it. His father said that I didn't have to open it then and he hung around for about another twenty minutes or so before leaving. As I turned from locking the door, I immediately found myself being strangled with both of his hands around my neck.

I couldn't move. All I could do was nothing but stand there until he decided to let me go or not. You see, I had learned from being almost strangled to death by him before, to not move.

Don't struggle. Don't scream.

Breathe as slow as possible.

Don't panic and whatever I do, *Don't look at him* while he strangled me.

That made him madder and that would result in a beat down. So, as I stood there with his hands around my neck and my eyes closed, all I could think about is nothing.

Thinking about nothing made the pain easier to bear.

I don't know how long he stood there with his hands around my neck, squeezing my throat while screaming and cursing at the top of his lungs about how he should kill me for being disrespectful and unappreciative to his father. When he finally loosened his grip on my neck, he asked me to answer his question (which I honestly didn't hear him ask). When I opened my mouth all I could do was scream which prompt him to punch me square in the face.

That Christmas, around my neck I wore the purple "choker" necklace that he had given me, a busted lip and a black eye.

All were Christmas gifts from my husband.

*****

"Wow!" exclaimed my daughter, "That lobster is huge and I bet all cooked and buttered up with some lemon juice squeezed all over it!!"

I just stood there and nodded. I had said that she can get what she wanted to eat. After all it was her birthday.

"*What do you think Mommy?*", *are you going to get...*", her voice trailed off.

"*I'm sorry. I forgot and was just caught up in the moment. We can go somewhere else and eat.*"

"*No, Baby Gurl, we're going to eat right here and you are going to order your lobster and whatever else you want to eat.*" I gave her a hug to re assure her that today was about celebrating her day and not being captive to the past.

As she began to tell me the history of how lobster became a main seafood staple, in the back of my mind I

THRIVER: My Story To Tell

thought about how much I hated the word lobster. The memories that it conjured up was too much for me and I almost found myself wanting to run out of the restaurant.

Mother's Day 1995, he insisted that we go to City Island. Not because I wanted to but because he wanted to. I said nothing because it wasn't my day. It was Mother's Day and it was his day. These were typical special occasions where it really was about him than anyone else.

It was *his* day to call and tell everyone that he was taking me to City Island for Mother's Day and that I was already getting on his last nerve by taking too long to get dressed. We ended up stuck in traffic on that bridge for about ninety minutes and he was not happy. He began to tell me that he was stuck in traffic because I wanted to go to City Island. I suggested that we find our way out of traffic and go home but he was not having it. After all, he had already made sure everyone knew that is where he would be.

After finally getting on the island and finding parking, we walked over to the Lobster House and waited again. He began to be rude and belligerent to the wait staff and I was embarrassed but knew better than to say anything. Once we were seated, he ordered lobster of course and when I said that I didn't eat lobster, he kicked me under the table. I had a choice, eat or don't eat. If I chose not to eat there would be hell to pay on that ride back and once I got home. I ate the damn lobster and everything that was on the plate. When the car got to that semi remote area heading back off the island, he stopped and slapped the living crap out of me. For being ungrateful he said.

I *never, ever* ate lobster again, never frequented the Lobster House again and the next time I went back to City

Island was fifteen years after I had left him. That was a typical holiday, I mean, horriday.

But that day with my daughter, however, was joyous. We ate, she lobster and me a Cesar salad with grilled chicken and we laughed and laughed and celebrated her day and her life.

*****

Those moments of sheer terror, chaos and blood shed were the norm for Christmas, Easter, Birthdays, Graduations, just any moment that should have been celebrated. If he wasn't terrorizing us in one way, he did in other ways. For two weeks, there were no incidents.
No threatening phone calls, no sitting outside the building, no leaning on the door buzzer. Nothing.
Then out of the blue he decides to show up so that he can take us down to the Halloween Parade. I didn't go trick or treating as a child or take my children out on Halloween. But there he was rousing up the children and there they were pleading to go. I believe that he got a kick out of telling them how I always ruin everything.
I gave in and we piled into his vehicle and drove into the city for the parade. Everything was going smoothly until he was driving us back home. The two older ones were still up and excited and laughing and talking about the parade. As the vehicle was coming down the FDR, he pulled over, got out, walked over to the passenger side and pulled me out then woke up the two little ones and told all of my children to get out of his vehicle. Eleven thirty at night at 96th Street on the FDR on the Halloween night. He never said a word and just casually got back into his vehicle and pulled off.

We stood right in that spot in shock for about fifteen minutes. I couldn't catch a taxi since I had no money. I had no clue what to do so we began to walk toward the train station.

As we were walking up toward Second Avenue, he pulled back up laughing, *"Trick or Treat!"* he yelled. Silently we climbed back into the vehicle, buckled up our seat belts and proceeded to head back up to the Bronx.

It was thirteen years later before I went back to that parade. I had to. It was part of my healing process.

I remember vividly several days after one of those horriday incidents, there was a knock at the door and as I approached the door, I heard someone remark that they were tired of coming here. When I opened it, there were two female cops from the local precinct standing there. They said that they were from the domestic violence unit and was checking up on me. I was handed an envelope with a letter from the local precinct stating that my address/household had been designated a domestic violence household. I had no idea what the heck they were talking about and no clue what domestic violence was but it sure wasn't me. I put it in the drawer with all of the other documents.

Crazy thing is that all of these years later, I still have every piece of paper relating to that time in my life. Every piece from every hospital. Every agency. Every realtor. Every petition. Every place I went for ......*help?*

12

IF I WERE YOU...

STOP ASKING ME WHY I STAYED. You would have had to been in my shoes to understand, and I had plenty of shoes to wear. They grounded me and kept me sane. *Literally.* They were my distraction from all that was happening and my feeling of being trapped. They were my happy place. I purchased them because in my mind I would be wearing one of them to walk right out of that door, out of that marriage. In my mind it seemed like it could happen. Maybe. One day.

But in reality, where was I going with all of those kids and no money? No one cared and everyone had their own stuff going on. Wait, there was one person who would help. She would keep my kids for two weeks while I tried to find a somewhere for us to go but she wanted to be paid and well, I had no money, not the amount that she was asking for.

I used to try to work and actually always managed to find employment but once I would show up with my face beaten and bruised, that would be the end of that. Eventually I stop looking to work and survived the best I could off of public assistance.

I will tell you and every person who has ever been abused will tell you the same. Leave and go where? Did I want to be beaten and damn near killed in front of my children?

Did I deliberately set out to be with someone so that I could be humiliated and violated?

When I was a little girl with dreams and goals, was one of them to become a victim of abuse and to live my life in fear while being blamed judged and ridiculed by society?

Absolutely not! I didn't stay because I wanted to be abused.

I aspired to be a Veterinarian then later a College Professor.

I can't imagine anyone, any woman, who stay because they actually liked being beaten and abused.

I didn't. Nor did the any person that I know personally or professionally who is or has been victimized.

With all of the town hall meetings, seminars, church functions, conferences, information being disseminated via social media and through outreach there is one thing that hasn't changed: That aged old question of *Why doesn't the victim leave? Why won't she just leave?* Victim Blaming.

*****

The counselor looked at me and said, *"When are you going to leave him?"*

I absolutely could not believe that she asked me that. Which means that she had not heard a word that I had said in the past twenty minutes. I looked at her then asked, *"And go where?"*

THRIVER: My Story To Tell

At that point in my life I had never been out of New York State. I didn't know how to drive. I had no means of support. No family. I had no idea and no concept of where I could even go. The farthest I had ever been was to high school out in Harlem. All of these years later, I realize that asking a person that is being abused 'why don't they leave' or 'when are they going to leave' is a victim blaming statement.

I became what service providers call, confrontational and asked her again, *"And Go where?."* By this time, I had become frustrated with the fact that I had wasted my time coming to see her just for her to ask me such a stupid question. She sat there looking down at me with this look *as if I* was wasting her time.

She then had the nerves to tell me that if I wasn't so angry then maybe I wouldn't be being beaten. Now as much as I didn't know about domestic violence or didn't understand how dire the situation was at that time, I was fully aware that what she said was unprofessional and that in her ignorance, she was blaming me, the victim for his actions.

After I told her off royally, *I knocked everything* off of her desk, vowed never to go back and stormed out of her office. I never did return and it was well over a decade before I sought the counsel of a therapist again.

Why didn't I leave? Let me ask you this, where was I going with no job and four children. To your house? Could I have come to your home and stayed until I was stronger, until I was healed, until my psychological issues were resolved. Until I realized that I was a victim of domestic violence?

No. I didn't think so.

I stayed.

And I tried to get help.

I applied for apartments.

I went to organizations that were supposed to assist people who were in my situation.

I went to local elected officials.

I was desperate to get out.

To no avail.

I went to his parole officer who served him with a copy of the Order of Protection after he pushed me down a flight of stairs.

Again.

I went to his parents.

I went to the church.

I told my children school and supplied them with a copy of the Order of Protection.

I went to get stitched up by doctors who never questioned how I ended up needing medical care.

I searched high and low.

To no avail.

So, Yes. I stayed.

I am guilty as charged.

I stayed.

I believed that he would change.

That the abuse would stop.

I trusted his word and myself that I was doing right by the marriage.

I also believed him when he said that it would be easy to kill me and then I would really be gone.

If you were in my shoes, *you would have stayed too.*

12A

BARRIERS

THE NUMBER ONE WRONG QUESTION TO ask a person who is being abused is *why don't you leave.* That assumes that the person being abused wants to be. It also blames the abused person for the action of the abuser. Not so and if you are curious as to why they stay, well, here are some reasons why they stay. Let's take a look at some of the barriers to leaving a relationship, partnership or marriage where there is an abusive partner.

<u>Barriers To Leaving An Abusive Partner</u>

LACK OF AFFORDABLE/PERMANENT HOUSING- This is three-fold. Abused persons choose not to leave because they cannot afford the expenses associated with todays' housing market. Also, many who go into shelters end up homeless for extended periods of time due to lack of affordable housing. Landlords may also blacklist the abused partner by referring to them as problem tenants. *Or how about this*, the victim is told that she has to take her abuser to Housing Court to have him removed from the apartment where he is beating her. Now *that* is a barrier.

THRIVER: My Story To Tell

FEAR-The abused knows the abuser better than anyone and knows exactly what he/she is capable of. The abuser uses intimidation, threats against family and friends, sexual and physical violence to instill fear. The fear of what could happen or what will happen (again) is one way that the abuser keeps the abused partner from leaving.
(That loaded pistol in my mouth gave me a reason to fear.)

CULTURAL- It is culturally normal that the men dominate the relationship. To leave would place the abused in the position of being ostracized by the rest of the community further isolating them.

TECHNOLOGY-In this modern age of all things computerized and information linked, *HOW* does an abused person leave when they can easily be tracked down. Not only is their information easily accessible via internet but so is their relatives. Name, addresses, phone numbers. It is not just about GPS anymore but a click of the mouse or the download of an app and the person is found. And in some cases murdered.

RELIGIOUS- Some spiritual beliefs dictate that the man is the head of the household and the woman is to submit. Also, some religions view divorce as a sin. Houses of worship counsels the abused to stay in the marriage attributing the violence to disobedience or what God says about suffering.

NO FINANCES-Some abusers control all of the finances making it impossible for the abused partner to leave the relationship. Some abused people are on fixed incomes and cannot afford to leave or move to another location. Others are financially dependent on the abuser. In addition, a person who has poor credit or credit history often have a difficult time finding a landlord willing to rent to them.

NOWHERE TO GO- Not all states /municipalities have emergency placement for abused women. For single women without children, there are even less options and this is also true for men that are being abused. Family members often don't want to get involved and will not let the victim and their children stay. Lack of bed space and shelter restrictions are also a factor.

HEALTH/MEDICAL NEEDS The abused partner may be covered by the abusers' medical insurance or may have a hidden illness. The abuser may also threaten to disclose the partners medical condition (HIV+, Hepatitis) forcing the partner to stay. The abuser may be their caregiver or medical proxy.

AGE- There are many who have been with their abuser for many years and believe that they are too old to start again or that no one would want them because of their age.

ACCESS TO A FIREARM-Abusers with access to firearms uses it to intimidate the victim to stay by threatening to harm the partner and/or their family.

CHILDREN-Some don't want their children to grow up without their father. Some choose to stay to keep their children in familiar surroundings and don't wish to disrupt their lives. Still others stay to shield the children from the abusive partner.

PETS- Some don't want to leave behind the family pet and there are very limited options for boarding or taking the pet(s) with them.

NO SUPPORT SYSTEM- Some stay due to lack of support system. They may have no family or friends to help them get through the process of leaving and rebuilding. Some also stay because their support system has turned their backs on them because they haven't left/won't leave. A support system is crucial for an abused person whether they choose to remain or not.

IMMIGRATION-Abused people who do not have citizenship believe that they do not have any options due to their immigration status. Also, the abuser will threaten to report the partner to the authorities.

BELIEVES THAT THE ABUSER WILL CHANGE- The abuser often promises to change during the course of the relationship.

EMOTIONAL ATTACHMENT- The person being abused is still invested emotionally in the abusive partner and often don't equate the abuse as wrong and/or don't identify as being a victim.

REVICTIMIZED BY SERVICE PROVIDERS- Some have left but returned back after being let down by the system in place to assist them.

WANT TO STAY BUT WANT THE ABUSE TO STOP- Some want to be with their partner for one reason or for many different reasons. They simply want the abuse to stop.

While these may not seem like valid reasons for an abused person to stay as opposed to leaving, *it is for them to decide* as they know their situation and their abuser better than you do.

People stay for one, some, many or maybe all of these reasons. They can all be barriers to leaving and not all are physical. I listed eighteen and was faced with nine. Yes, *I stayed for nine out of eighteen of the barriers.* It was necessary and important that I included this in this book and that I took the time to break it down. This list is by no means complete

Questioning why the victim doesn't leave is victim blaming. The impact of this statement makes the abused person question what did they do wrong.

Victim blaming shames the abused person and if they have kids it shames the kids. It recreates the fear, enables the abuse to continue the abuse and it re victimizes the victim. It is done by family, friends and society. It allows everyone outside of the abuse *to not* take any ownership to what is happening and empowers the abuser.

Victim blaming also strips the abused person of any dignity and self-respect they may have.

Yes, dignity and self -respect.

Do you really believe that abused persons don't respect themselves? It is the abuser who is being disrespectful.

THRIVER: My Story To Tell

Do you know how much inner strength it takes to get out of the bed and walk out into the world all beat up. That's being dignified.

Do you know how humiliating it is to open your door the next morning and step out into the community that everyone knows your situation? That you are being beaten?

That's facing the world head on in spite of how judgmental and disrespectful it is toward you.

Actually, it is the abuser and those that blame, shame and judge the victim that don't have any self-respect

Was I embarrassed by my situation? Yes. That didn't make me pitiful or weak. That didn't make me stupid for staying. It didn't mean that I had no respect for myself.

I was operating under hostile conditions.

While I was clueless *how* to love myself, that did not mean I was any of the nasty, mean, negative and derogatory names that society bestowed upon me. I got up, got dressed and handled my business. Whatever that may have been, and I handled it as dignified and respectful as I possibly could, considering my circumstances being beaten, dejected and ridiculed. I still had to handle business.

I still had to take my kids to school, to their doctors' appointment, to their afterschool program. They still needed their laundry done and food to eat. They still needed to go to church and to the playground.

The only undignified persons were the ones gossiping, judging and blaming me for being the victim of a crime.

If you have to ask, try asking, What is preventing you from leaving? and when you do please keep this is mind:

Telling and demanding someone to leave, in reality places them in more harm. *In order to empower victims and survivors to move forward, any decision they make must be theirs. Even if they wish to stay.* After all, they know their abuser better than you and they knows what goes on behind their closed door.

Please stop TELLING victims to leave. Please.

You don't know what is *really* happening to them behind closed doors. And, please, stop telling people that are being abused, to not be afraid. They Know their reality.

They know exactly *what their abuser is capable of.*

If you truly want to help them, please stop saying those two things.

*****

In cases where victims do escape, there are many that are subjected to Separation Violence where the violence itself often *increases after* and the victim, especially women, are more likely to be murdered at this point then at any other time.

Although separated from the abuse, the abuser may also utilize the court system as a way of staying connected to the victim through child support, child visitation orders and also by refusing to sign divorce papers.

Through court related abuse and harassment, many abusers are able to torment the victim even after they have left.

Escaped.

Mine did.

For two long excruciating years.

13

SUMMER 95

˙

IN AUGUST 1995, TWO MAJOR INCIDENTS happened. The first, on my Big Girls' tenth birthday and the second eight days later was perhaps for me the events that led me to totally disconnect from people.

August 13, 995 was a precursor to one of the most unforgettable incidents of all the ten years.

Exactly eight days after that a series of events would forever change my children and myself.

However, this day, August 13, 1995, started out like any other, hot summer day with the exception that it was my oldest daughters' tenth birthday.

*****

Double digits I used to say. A big deal for her and for me.

Everyone was excited because her birthday party going to be at the park.

A birthday barbeque.

We packed up and drove down to the park. Which was only three blocks away and when we got there he didn't like the spot and decided to pick up the picnic table and move it to another location.

Well, why did I say let's just stay here? He swung that table so fast and cracked me on the side of my face in front of everyone. No one said a word.

As the blood began to trickle down my face and the children started screaming, he dropped the table and came toward me, I grabbed the baby stroller and we, my three older kids and I, began running back home. By the time I got to the building, he was jumping out of his van and there was nothing could I do but try to get in the building.

Now on this hot, hot August day, it seemed like everyone, I mean *everyone* was either outside or looking out of their window and then there was me. I grabbed the baby out of her stroller and as I went to run he grabbed her two little feet and there we are in the middle of the sidewalk tugging back and forth on this poor little baby and blood falling from my head.

No one said a word. But there stood my neighbors watching that scene play itself out like an episode on television. Long before reality tv, there was my life for all to see.

I don't know who call them but when the cops came they threatened to arrest us both and take all of my children. He told them who his father was and they told him to let go of the baby and take a walk and that is exactly what he did. He let go of my baby's feet then left. Then they left. They never even addressed why I was bleeding from my head or why we were in a tug of war, literally, with the baby who had just turned three. They just simply left.

As I gathered my distraught children and walked into my building, no one held the door for me, no one said a word. It was just another day, another horriday and that is how my daughter spent her tenth birthday. He had completely ruin any future birthdays for her. And she never forgave me.

Eight days later…….

*****

Eleven thirty pm, Children screaming and blood everywhere. All I remembered after he punched me in the face was waking up in the ambulance with my then twelve-year old son leaning over me saying that it was going to be alright.

He had called about nine thirty to say that he was heading in and asked if the kids were in bed. I said yes and hung up. I knew from the sound of his voice that he had been drinking and that it was going to be a long night. If I didn't open the door, he would be waiting outside when the sun came up. He would be waiting for me to step out from behind that closed door. And there would be another public beat down for all the neighbors to see.

Fear kicked in.

I got up and went into the living room to wait for him and fell asleep on the couch. Once he got there, all hell broke loose.

He came inside and asked why was I up and actually I didn't say anything. You see, I didn't know what to say.

Anything could be the wrong thing. So, I said nothing.

He grabbed my right wrist and started softly saying, *'It's okay Baby. You can talk to me".*

"I was just waiting for you", I said.

Then he asked if I wanted him to leave.

I became terrified. Trick question.

Once again, I said nothing and he began chiding with me to answer.

I knew that if I said no, he would call me a liar then beat me up.

I knew if I said yes, he would beat me up.

He asked again and as I turned to face him, he cracked me in the mouth with the hand that he wore that huge diamond ring on. The next thing I remember hearing was two things, my niece screaming at him, *"What are you doing to my Aunt DD!!"*, and then, my sons' voice in the ambulance.
Whatever happened in between him hitting me in my face and me waking up in the ambulance, I still have no memory twenty odd years later. I don't remember at what point my finger was broken or how I ended up with multiple contusions on my face.

I opened my eyes to a bright light overhead, the sounds of sirens and my son staring into my face.

"It's going to be okay Mommy. Everything is going to be okay." We were in an ambulance and I don't even remember which hospital I was taken to.

What I didn't know in that moment is what my face looked like. I had no idea how damaged it was and I believe that was the turning point for my son. I believe that night killed him and all the humanity inside of him. I also believe that what occurred after that destroyed his belief in all things good.

August 22, the morning after he punched me in the face, cracked my mouth wide open and broke my finger in the process. *I tried to leave again.*

We try to leave, that very same day after I got back from the hospital. First, I spent the entire day at the Bronx Criminal Court with Victim Services, taking pictures and being interviewed. (Thank God for the worker who gave me one of the Polaroids). About twenty-two stitches inside and out of my top lip and multiple contusions on my forehead and a broken finger (that is one "fight" I don't remember much).

He was even able to walk right up in the back where I was. My head was down and I thought I heard him say my name. When I looked up, there he was!

I started screaming for dear life and he ran. By the time the court officers and workers came to where I was placed to sit, he was gone. I was told that I must have been dreaming, that he was unable to get back there. That was not true then and is not true now.

We, my children and my then sixteen -year old niece who was living with me, we were sent to EAU Emergency Assistance Unit, NYC emergency housing and when we finished getting processed it was about eleven at night.

There is now a new building that sits there now but the old one was only one story with a basement level. The block is on an incline so as one walked down the block you or anyone could look directly into the place and see the families that were there…waiting for their turn to be sent or taken into a shelter.

That night after being processed my family was escorted to the basement area where the lights had already been turned down and the other families were asleep on the floor. The employee who took us down there approached a family that was lying up under the window where her family was protected from being seen by anyone passing by. She woke this woman up and asked if we could rest there and that mother flipped out. She began cussing so loudly that others woke up and we just stood there even more ashamed than what we were.

It was a nightmare and I was in shock and couldn't believe that even with the injuries that I had sustained that we were expected to sleep on the floor. We found an open spot in the middle of the floor and when morning came, I took my family and went back home.

It was a mess and I could barely function. My entire body was in such pain and I had no choice but to press through so that we could get out of there. I worked with Victim Services from home and I was given a letter stating that due to the size of my family, they were unable to assist me. It was approximately three weeks later when I received a call informing me that there was placement at a domestic violence shelter in Long Island.

We were so happy!

We were going to be so far from him!

It was over!

We pack our most precious items, one backpack for everyone and went to get placed but when we got there, I was informed that my son could not go. The shelter with the opening did not allowed male children over the age of ten due to their propensity to become batterers.

That is exactly what I was told.

My twelve-year old son could not go into the shelter because he was over ten years of age. He was a minor being penalized for what an adult had done. For a crime that he did not commit.
I was also told that there were no other available beds so if I wanted that placement, I had to make arrangements for my son because he couldn't go with us.
My brain couldn't make sense of what I was hearing. I must have heard her wrong. I was standing there with the brace still on my hand to support the broken finger, the bruises on my face had not healed, the scar tissue fresh and hanging from my upper lip and five crying children and was trying to make sense of what was being said..

The look on my sons' face will forever stay with me.
This kid who learned how to cook, clean and take care of his sisters not only because I was being beaten but also because the system that was supposed to help us became our Secondary Abuser.

No amount of pleading would change the fact.

We had no choice but to go back.

I would not abandon my son.

And so, we went back to Five Seventy Five East One Hundred and Fortieth Street and remained in that abusive situation for another three years.
And this is a practice that continues today. Placement for victims and survivors is at a premium. Those

in the business of domestic violence shelters make the rules and policies that impact the lives and jeopardize the safety of the families who are ready to leave and more often than not, it is the children that pays the ultimate price.

These are also our teens and young adults who leave home in search of someplace safe and somewhere to feel wanted with many ending up in gangs, being trafficking, becoming pregnant, hooked on drugs or infected with diseases.

These are many of the children who ends up in trouble with the law, like my son. These are many of the children who end up addicted to drugs and/or alcohol, like one of my daughters.

These are the children who grow up to hate themselves and become self-destructive, like another one of my daughters who self-mutilated for many years.

And the ones who outwardly don't, suffer inwardly.

I *personally* know lawyers, doctors, clergy, teachers, law enforcement, domestic violence providers and many other professionals who were once children living in households where there was abuse or who were themselves victims of intimate partner violence.. Yes, they, like me was able to move forward and just like me, inwardly they will always bear the traumatic memories.

My children, even as adults, still bear the emotional scars. They are four of hundreds of millions of now grown children who very lives took a turn for the worse because they lived in a household watching their mother being beat with no means of escape.

THRIVER: My Story To Tell

This is true to my story and how my children and I were forced to learn to survive within the abuse.

We did not learn how to be helpless.

We returned and learned to adapt to the situation, but *we did not* learn how to be helpless.

There was no time to learned "how to be" helplessness or anytime to be helpless.

We learned *HOW* to survive in that environment the best that we could and to cope with the abuse the best that we knew how with the person who was terrorizing us knowing that we had no other options.

Those were the Best practices that we applied to our inconceivable and inescapable circumstances.

And as the ripples began to cascade over our heads and turn into crashing waves, we were drowning and all that we could do was try to not swallow the water.

That, was our Safety Planning.

14

PREYED UPON

During the bulk of 1995-98, we did not live together. He basically lived as he pleased, coming and going whenever. Yet he knew every move I made. He knew everywhere I went and when I went. He would even show up early in the morning at the laundry while I was there. After all, at this point we were stuck.

Being stalked while being abused is the absolute most challenging and terrifying thing in the world next to almost being murdered.

For me it was.

With the violence, you kind of have an idea of what's going to happen. You can kind of gauge the situation and you learned what to do or say or wear or not. You know who you are dealing with and to a certain extent, *what* you are dealing with.

That is just not the case with stalking.

You just don't know what is going to happen next, where your abuser is going to show up at or how he is going to show up. You don't know if he is watching you or if he has paid someone to watch you.

You don't know what to expect when you are at the laundry, the supermarket or picking up the kids from school.

I didn't know.

I

              Just

                                don't

know.

That is a no way to live.

His threats became so frightening that I was afraid to leave my home for two straight weeks. Make no mistake, it wasn't just his verbal threats that kept me inside for those two weeks.

I knew *exactly* what he was capable of.

He had access to a gun and I believed that he would kill me just as he had said he would. He had access to bullets. That is the same gun he loaded some bullets in and placed in my mouth. Neither my babies or I left the apartment. I had resorted to covering all of the windows with sheets so that he would not know when I turn my lights on at night.

It was one of those times that I had called the cops and that set him off and for that I would pay if I step one foot outside. We literally stayed inside for two weeks until I was forced to go outside. I had no choice. Had to take my chance. There were four kids and no more food.

That was another long summer.

Another incident of him stalking me was just so genius (I am being facetious). He would have dozens of red roses delivered to my mothers' house and to the children school. At first, everyone just thought that I was the luckiest wife and how they wish that their husband would have flowers delivered to their children school. However, my reaction to seeing these flowers sitting in the main office would make me nauseous. I knew the true meaning why they were sent. I understood the message loud and clear: *I am in control, I have access and you have no win. I can get to you anytime, anywhere I wanted.*

Now each time the flowers came, I would 'donate" them to the school. That's right, I would leave them right there on that counter top in the main office. School personnel then started viewing me as an ungrateful wife so my relationship with the school changed and I was more than happy when my children completed school there.

The funny thing about those flowers and those people in that school is that they knew about the abuse. There was an active order of protection that had been served to him and a copy was given to the school for him to stay away from my children. Although beaten and abused, I did not hide the bruises. They knew. Yet the school fell for it hook, line and sinker and I too, fell right in line by refusing to "accept his apology" thus becoming the bad guy.

The stalking and the flowers were all part of the manipulation. Both were designed to cast the victim, *me,* as the partner with the problem while making the abuser out to be the abused. To the general public, the abuser typically presents themselves as good guys. They're clean cut, well- spoken and well liked. They say all the right things and people often find them charming and personable. They are the favorite deacons in church, the guy who plays with the neighbors' kids, the dude who always have a smile and a nice word for everyone. They often appear to have the perfect family. They are the guys with a nine to five or a city job that is always on time, reliable and everyone can depend on.

My ex-husbands' outside persona did not match his behind closed doors persona and when he discovered that the cops and the courts were not going to do anything, he was free to be himself in public and the beatings went from behind closed doors to in public.

He was a master manipulator.

She doesn't appreciate all that he does for her and those kids.

She always has an attitude.

She's anti social and doesn't speak to anyone.

And as far as everyone was concerned, because of my attitude and ungratefulness, it was my fault.

Even though everyone who knew us, knew that *he was beating me.*

15

IMPRISONED

BEING IMPRISONED CAN TAKE ON SEVERAL forms. A person can be imprisoned physically, in jail or held captive against their will. A person can also be imprisoned in their mind due to mental health issues or psychological abused and imprisoned by trauma.

I have been imprisoned in two of those ways. First as a prisoner of the psychological abuse that I endured by my abuser. The fear and the pain inflicted by the threats to kill me was as real as the beatings and the sexual assaults. The intimidation and mental abuse so damaging that there were periods of times that I couldn't sleep and couldn't eat. Literally could not eat and at one point weighed less than one hundred pounds at thirty years of age. That never deterred him and it didn't change what he was doing.

Then by the fear, the drama and the trauma that had settled in. Couldn't function independent of what he said.

My indecision to make decisions were based on his reaction to my decisions which was made or not made based how he would react to the decisions I made…or not.

It is almost laughable that the professionals that I sought help from couldn't help me because *to them* my fears were irrational and unreasonable. It didn't matter that I bore the scars of the abuse.

Who do you trust when the people who you should trust minimizes and invalidates your reality and your experiences of abuse that leaves you shattered, confused, in despair.

It wasn't that I was blaming anyone for not helping us or throwing myself some pity party.

No! I was angry as hell that I was following all of the rules and regulations and playing by the rules and no would help. Plus, the fact that I was in a lot of emotional pain.

And I was tired.

I was already on lock down, so I did the next best thing.

I put a wall.

I built my own gated community.

Then I added a moat.

I became the dragon that kept away all unwanted visitors.

Without realizing what I was doing I had locked myself away from everyone and in attempt to protect myself, I imprisoned myself. I was Safety Planning. *Again.*

I also want to speak about women who are imprisoned for killing their partner after being abused. It is a topic that is rarely discussed and there are no real stats on. The majority of these women former abusers were known to the criminal justice system, yet they were not protected and eventually found themselves in a fight to the death. The law calls their 'not guilty, self-defense plea', premeditated murder since as far as the courts is concerned, all the woman had to do was leave.

Yes. Just leave. (sounds familiar.... doesn't it)

Even though the statistics that everyone look at that reports that a woman is more likely to be murdered when attempting to leave or within the first year of leaving (escaping) there is little to no consideration of the prior and often long term abuse that she suffered.

How can she, how does she, well, leave?

That begs the question, how does the victim now become the offender if there is documented evidence that she was being abused. The laws that are supposed to protect victims only protect the abusers when it comes down to intimate partner violence.

I still don't understand *why* the words "intimate relationship" changes the scope of the law when the same crimes of assault and battery or sexual assault or strangulation that is committed on a complete stranger versus a person's partner, former partner, child's mother or father is treated as a crime. A "real" crime.

If the law is about justice and making a person whole, why are there double standards because sex is or was involved between the two parties?

THRIVER: My Story To Tell

This strikes very close to home for me because *I could have* been one of those imprisoned women.

Yes. Me. Doreen G. Lesane.

One Mothers' Day, I blogged this on my social media page:

As the woman walked away after wishing me a "Happy Mothers' Day', I shook my head wistfully and thought about all of the mothers sitting imprisoned. I thought abought their children and their grandchildren. I thought about the loved ones who had passed from this life and into the next and I thought about how the hustle and bustle and shopping and cooking and planning and laughing and hugging and tweeting and posting and...business as usual.

And how, as these mothers abused and battered and broken and victimized and revictimized and now...forgotten by friends and families who have simply moved on, stopped writing, stopped visiting or just never wrote and never visited or....just can't afford the expenses of the trip.

I thought about the children who watched their mothers being beat then watched their mothers get arrested for defending themselves or their children.

I thought about those children who now watched for 5, 10, 15 years as their mothers grow old behind bars...convicted of trying not to be killed by their abuser.

And as I thought about them, it forced me to think about how I almost ended up a mother behind bars just because I was being abused.

And so this Mother's Day, I won't be primping, shopping, cooking, or celebrating. I won't be posting or laughing or any of that.

I will be praying for all of the mothers and for those who are now grandmothers, that someone, somewhere remember them.

THRIVER: My Story To Tell

I will be praying for their children and their grandchildren.

And I will be thanking God that He spared me from that fate.

*****

Honestly, that could have been me. I could have been one of the thousands of women that are incarcerated for protecting themselves. There is a day that comes and without even being aware of what transpires, that in the heat of that moment, it becomes *more than* survival.

It just happens.

Really.

It all happened so fast.

I did not see him anywhere when I walked into the block where I lived.

I was in a different neighborhood about five zip codes uptown on the other side of time.

We did not live together. We did not hang out. We did not have discussions of any type. We were not friends. We were not co-parenting. I did not communicate with his family. But he continued to torment me.

Because he could.

THRIVER: My Story To Tell

This particular day, I left work early and went to the realtor but since I didn't have my social security card, he wouldn't process the application. I told him that I would be back in ninety minutes. *I was trying to move again.*

I made it home and sprinted up the flight of stairs to my unit, unlocked the door and as I turned to lock it, there he was.

No, seriously, *there he was.*

He had his foot wedged in it so that I couldn't close it. He had slipped into the building right behind me and followed me up the flight of stairs.

We began struggling at the door and he pushed his way in. I just remember screaming at the top of my lungs. It wasn't a scream for help but one of pure rage and as he pushed his way into the apartment, I ran further inside and began throwing things at him, shouting at him to leave.

Get out!! Get out!! Get out!!

Get out!! Get out!! Get out!!

Over and over again, I kept screaming for him to get out. To leave me alone!

He didn't and began to laugh and call me stupid, said that I was bugging out for no reason.

Told me to shut up. Then he started moving further inside toward me. I grabbed a large book , threw that at him and then *I saw it.*

Hanging on the wall.

I ran, grabbed it and as I started charging towards him, I began to scream and shout.

"Get out!"

"Get Out!"

"Get Out!"

He started to laugh.

"You stupid little Bitch, you wouldn't dare.", he chuckled.

I swung it.

But it never connected because my son had grabbed my arm and my oldest daughter grabbed the other arm and my two younger daughters were holding me around the waist.
I never saw or heard them come out of their rooms. The entire time that they were restraining me all that I could do was scream and struggle to break free. And scream. And scream.
"You crazy Bitch!" he yelled.
"I'm going to call the cops on you!" he yelled as he bolted down the stairs.

They let me go and we all fell to the floor and began crying. Talk about chaos and trauma.

The cops never came.

Thank God. Truly.

I lost it and was just so done with this man harassing me and tormenting me and stalking me and just doing what he wanted to do.

In that moment and *in that moment*, I almost lost everything because no one would help me.

No one.

Not his parents.

Not the cops.

Not the courts.

No one.

This person who had harassed me, tormented me, beat me, beat my son, psychologically battered my children, stalked me and raped me for over a period of eight and a half years and who had just pushed himself into my home had carte blanche by the criminal justice system to do so.
Because he could since the laws that are written protects the offender when it comes to domestic violence. Because society blames the victim and the abuser gets a free pass.
It was insane the number of times that the police had been called concerning this one person.
It was insane that there was documentation that this person was committing criminal acts yet free to roam the streets freely and terrorize me and my children.

It was insane that I was a victim of a crime, yet he had more rights than I did because nothing was being done to stop his criminal acts against me.

Was the life of myself and my children worthless to the powers that be?

In that moment, I was insane and lost all common sense. Yes, I had lost my mind in that moment. I lost track of time and I was insane enough in that moment to stop that person from bothering me ever again.

And no.

I didn't think about it.

It just happened.

Almost found myself arrested and imprisoned with all of the other women who Just

    Could

                        Not

          Take

     It   Anymore

and I was in the fight of my life....*for my life.*
Looking back, I thank God that my children were home. Not only because they stopped me but also because he could have taken it and killed me......and would have gotten away with it.

The criminal justice system calls it pre-meditated.

It is not.

It really just happens in that moment.

Your mind goes blank.

My mind went blank.

The only thought was I wanted him out of my house.

Hurting him was the last thing on my mind.

I just wanted him out of my place.

He would not leave and actually started to laugh, like it was funny that I was standing there screaming.

It is a fight for one's life. It was a fight for my life.

I call the criminal justice system a failure when it comes to abused women. The penalties that these women suffered are disproportionate to what a man gets when he kills his intimate or former partner.

More often than not, the women that ends up in prison have suffered extensive abuse at the hands of their abusers and the criminal justice system has records of this.

The abuse perpetrated on me was recorded, well documented and well known yet had I touched him that day, it would have nullified what he had done to me all of those years prior to *that one moment* and I would have gone to prison.

It took me almost two weeks to process what had happened and what could have happened.

He stalked me, stood outside where I lived until I arrived home, followed me upstairs and then forced his way into my apartment *but if it* would have connected…..

Everyone always says, why did she stay, she should have left.

The real question is why does the criminal justice system continue to allow abusers, serial batterers to plea down the charges and then walk free with no consequences to the damage that they have perpetrated on their victims *and the children* that are present during those assaults.

It is not about why do victims stay as it is about the barriers that prevent them from leaving, including the laws that allow abusers to walk free to abuse again.

I didn't just survive domestic violence.

I survived going to prison because I was a victim of domestic violence.

I am not an ex-convict but I was once imprisoned.

Held captive and in chains by the laws that forbade me to defend myself against a criminal that was double my weight and almost a full foot taller than I.

THRIVER: My Story To Tell

I was in solitary confinement by the laws that was written to protect me *and* would have been used against me. Laws unenforced with as much power as a nursey rhyme sung to a newborn.

I was stripped of my rights to defend myself, to live free and unafraid, to care for my children or pursue my dreams.

I was imprisoned with the inability to be free *not because* of a crime I committed but because of the crime being committed against me.

I became a criminal without committing a criminal act only because I was a victim of Intimate Partner Violence and for no other reason.

Intimate Partner Violence and Rape are the only two crimes where it is the victims fault, *even though they are victims.*

How ironic.

16

LAUNDRY TIME

THREE MONTHS AFTER THAT INCIDENT IT was laundry time.

"We need to leave now before the laundry gets crowded. Let's go."

"*Now.*"

*****

After I had cleaned the apartment and went grocery shopping, the two younger girls stood downstairs in the front of the house while my son and my older daughter helped bring the two carts downstairs. Dusk was falling and I wanted to be home before it became dark.

We walked to the corner then crossed the street and walk toward the laundromat but didn't stop. We proceeded to walk another six blocks and then stopped at the double building, entered it, got on the elevator to the third floor and when we got out, I pulled out the keys, opened the door and once my children entered the apartment, I locked it and we were free.

Prior to the last assault, I had already begun to plan our escape.

THRIVER: My Story To Tell

I was actually apartment hunting when he stalked me that January afternoon that almost ended up with me almost imprisoned. Our trip to the laundry was really our exit plan. One block south. One block west. Another three blocks south. (Past the Laundromat) Make a right at the corner. Three blocks west, crossed the street and two blocks east.

Ten blocks to freedom.

*****

That same year, six weeks after that other incident, there was that *last time* he ever touched me. March 27, 1998. There he was, standing in front of the house, again, with a single red rose and the dog hanging out of the car. He was parked directly in front of the entrance. No choice but to walk pass him. As I walked across the street, I felt absolutely nothing. I was so disgusted and it took all of my strength not to tell him off.

As the baby and I got closer and he reached for her, she pulled back behind my legs away from his hand. He leaned closer toward me and held out the rose. I kept walking without saying a word.

"*Hey Baby, I came to see you*", he said all nonchalantly.

My plans were different. In my mind all I had to do was make it up those four short steps, so I kept walking, up one stair then another and finally the last step.

I almost made it.

Just before I got to the door, I was viciously slammed against the wall and he began to curse at me while strangling me with all his might. I did something I had never done before.

I looked him straight in his face.

Then I began struggling to get loose and as I did, I saw both the baby and the dog run up into the house and up the flight of stairs. As I begin to lose the struggle and lose consciousness, I heard a thumping noise and out came my then fifteen-year old son with the bat.

I like to say and it is my belief that the dog, Top, went and got my son. Although my Baby Gurl had ran upstairs, it was only the fact that the dog went upstairs as well, that my son knew *he* was around.

As I heard my son jumping down the stairs, I could have sworn that the dog came down as well barking at him. He released his grip from my neck, slammed my head into the wall and ran toward his car with my son chasing him and the dog barking.

As he tried to avoid my son who was swinging the bat at him, he attempted to grab his dog, but the dog was barking and running around.

I laid on the stoop gasping for air. I just could not believe that once again he assaulted me and to make matters worse, my neck was bleeding from the ring that he had on his. Somehow, the side with the diamonds was pressed on my neck and the pressure had broken the skin.

The same ring that was on his hand when he busted my face up that night three years ago.

After what seemed an eternity, he managed to grab the dog and get into his car and my son finally came and helped me upstairs where we began searching for my five-year old daughter.

We found her sitting under the table in the kitchen crying hysterically and as we tried to reach for her, she pulled back and what she said I will never forget.

"If I was never born then my father wouldn't be beating you."

A five-year old child blaming herself for her fathers' action. My Baby Gurl. Not only did that haunt me for years, she became suicidal later in life.

It was also this particular incident that began to change my perspective on many things, *including the police*. Up to this point, he had never been arrested or taken into custody for assaulting me or my son.

The detective assigned to the case said that she was going to arrest him, which I did not believe her.

She did. The case hung out in the criminal justice system for two years. I was never asked to testify. I was never asked if I wanted to be involved. In my mind I thought that he would be locked up for what he had done to me all of those years. *I was wrong. That is not how the criminal justice system works.*

Eventually all he ended up with is ten days in jail and a court fine. That's it. Ten days or one day for each year he abused us.

*****

No one knew where we were.

We entered a completely empty three-bedroom apartment with the clothes on our backs, two shopping carts of clothes, some food, their bookbags for school and the family cat Diamond.

The next morning, I got up and jumped on the train to Third Avenue to go and see if the store manager at Furniture King would give me credit for some beds.

When I arrived, I asked to speak with the manager and when he came out, I pulled out my uncashed paycheck from work and told him my situation. I left my husband and have a new place for my kids but don't have any furniture and need beds for them.

I didn't have any idea what a credit score or what the heck he meant when he asked how was my credit. Then I had to tell him why I left my then husband. Instead of taking the whole check like I offered him, he afforded me the opportunity to walk away with a bed for my son, a white day bed for my oldest daughter and a white bunkbed for the two younger ones to be delivered the next day and he didn't charge a delivery fee. He said the monies that you didn't spend here use it to get bedding and that is exactly what I did.

It took me six months to pay for those beds but it didn't matter.

We were safe.

My bed? No. I didn't get one. I didn't need one.

I made a pallet on the floor with my clothes and a blanket right behind my bedroom door and that is where I slept every night for six months until their beds were paid for and their bedrooms transformed into real rooms so that they could begin to live a normal childhood.

For the first time in ten years, we could sleep through the night without being afraid that when he arrived, the furniture would be violently destroyed by my body being thrown into them or him smashing them in a fit of rage. There would be none of that. We could prepare for bed, turn off the lights and honestly close our eyes and rest.

For the first time in ten years, my children would be able to have a violent free and joy filled birthday party with no cakes being smashed or me trying to hold the blood in my mouth after getting slapped for laughing at a joke.

For the first time in ten years, I could decide to get up and go out without being stalked. Without being tormented. Without the fear of what was going to happen when I get back because I had the wrong clothes on, was gone too loo long, was on the wrong side of town, talking to the wrong people or had taken too long to cook.

For the first time in ten years, I could walk out of my building and I did not have to worry about him sitting parked in front of the place I called home.

*****

I got up every morning, got dressed, got them up and ready for school and walked out of that apartment just like I just had the best rest of my life on a queen-sized bed.

Some mornings I would wake up and find all of my babies lying on the floor next to me. And for about three years, no one knew where we were. Not where I lived. Worked. Did laundry. Where I purchased our groceries. No one knew which schools my children attended or which playgrounds they played on. No one, anywhere we went, knew our names or where we were from. The people in the immediate neighborhood, the stores knew me only as the Angry lady with four kids. My two oldest children were not allowed to bring friends home and that is how we lived for the first three years after escaping from the abuse.

I didn't trust anyone. Not family and had long ago, discarded any friends. Anyone and everyone who knew him was no longer a part of my life, even if they had met him through me. I was not going to take the chance of him finding me this time or ever again.

It wasn't until I disappeared May of 1998 after he was arrested for the first time ever for assaulting me, that I was free physically. *So I thought.*

He continued to stalk me by visiting everyone he thought would tell him my whereabouts and when he couldn't find me, he tried to flush me out.

I was relatively new with the then New York City Board of Education as a paraprofessional, just under a year. He knew that I worked in some school in Harlem but wasn't too sure where at this point. As a substitute in my first year, I went from school to school.
And once I became permanent, I continued to find valid reasons to be transferred from one school to another, then from one borough to the next. I was not going to be found by him.
What started the series of transfer was one phone call. After arriving home from work one day, I checked my answering machine for messages and had only one.

"Hello This is Mrs. Olgivie. There is a matter that I need to discuss with you. Please call me as soon as you get this message." The phone number she left was her home phone number. I dialed the number and when she answered the phone I was not surprised at all at what I heard.

"I am glad that you returned my call so promptly. I received a call from One Ten Livingston Street who said that they received a call from District Seventy-Five. We were informed that you are unfit to be working around children due to the fact that you are a stripper and abuses your children."
" Mrs. Olgivie, I assure you that none of that is true and as a matter of fact, I can tell you that my husband who has been beating me is the person that made that call."

"Really, she said, *" from what we are being told is that if we don't fire you, that the person is going to go to the Daily News and say that we hired a stripper and child abuser to work in the public school system."*

"As I told you, that was my husband. I left him and he doesn't know where I am and have documentation to prove what I am saying."

"Well, either you have those documents to prove what you are saying or don't bother coming back to work," and then hung up before I could say another word.

The next day I reported to her with my documents and several days later she called me into her office and gave me what was a copy of a letter that was going to my employee file. It stated in part that the New York City Board of Education had conducted an investigation into the matter and also spoke with my then father in law who corroborated my story. It detailed that my then husband had threatened to go to the Daily News with false allegations about me and also stated that if he was caught on any school property that he would be arrested for trespassing.

I had also heard through the grapevine that during this time period, he had blown up and posted numerous *personal* pictures of me throughout the neighborhood and also visited everyone home that he could think of looking for me and pleading with others for them to relay messages or tell him where I was.

But no one knew where I was because I deliberately did not tell anyone. And what no one knew but me is that every opportunity I got to transfer out of a school, I did. I didn't know who he knew and my past dictated that no one was going to help me but me.

I was in straight up stay on the move mode. There was no turning back this time.

And in the midst of all that was going on, the divorce was granted. I was free physically and with the divorce being granted by default, Cruel and Inhumane treatment the judge said, I was free.

It was exhilarating and overwhelming at the same time.

We finally had a safe place to call home.

And we lived there for six drama filled years.

Me angry. Them angry.

And filled with Trauma and Drama.

We were safe from him. Somewhat.

But not safe from the memories and what the memories stirred up.

For a while, I was able to put all of that behind me.

17

FOREVER AND TWO DAYS

LIFE IS REALLY NOT EVER THE same after trauma. While there can be Life after Domestic Violence, it is never the same. It improves with time and how one views it afterwards makes all the difference. Acceptance is the word that comes to mind. However, there is a degree of cautiousness that I personally approach life with now so that I don't find myself in *any* unhealthy relationship.

Personally, professionally or spiritually.

Although I had finally escaped that madness my process was not smooth or easy and I was filled with anger, and mistrust and I was deliberately isolating myself. There were people who offered to help, for a fee of course although I was drowning and could barely keep my head above water, including financially.

There are situations where I could have definitely been killed because of my mouth and my reaction to things. On the outside and in the public, I was mean and nasty and took no shorts from anybody. If I felt threatened in any way or if I thought someone was trying to get over, watch out because I had more than a few choice words for you. Everyone around me called me the Angry Lady with Four Kids.

Yes, I was angry but didn't know why.

I was angry and it showed in my walk, the way I interacted with people, even at school. I would not back down from a debate and often found myself in tears.

No one was allowed to mess with me or my children.

No One.

I remembered that on one occasion I called out from work and just stayed home. After picking up my two youngest daughters and settling them in, I went back to lying across the couch. I heard the door open and my Big Girl come in cursing and screaming at someone. As I got up and inched toward the door, she was still telling someone to stop playing and give her the umbrella. I heard a guys' voice telling her to come out of the apartment and get it and as she turned around and saw me, I put my fingers over my lips and snatched the door wide opened.

There stood two of the neighborhood thugs now with their mouth wide open." *Excuse me, but what is the problem and why are you standing in front of MY door ".*

For a second neither said a word. You see, they didn't know that I was home but knew that my son had been arrested a couple of months ago. I then proceeded to snatch the umbrella out of his hand and tell him to stay away from my daughter and my door, unless he wanted problems. I didn't mince my words and used a lot of colorful ones.

He stammered that he wasn't looking for any problems and was just playing with her, that him and my son were friends. I told him he was friends with my son. *Not my daughters.* I also said that I would be explaining this to him and his little buddies just one time…stay away from my daughters. Or there will be a problem.

Now what was so crazy about this encounter is that everyone in the surrounding neighborhood was afraid of this person and his reputation. My son had warned me of him and my son had also warned him about staying away from his sisters. But I wasn't afraid of him or anyone else.

I had smelled death on my very body three different times and was not going to let anyone ever control me or mess with my children. Not even him.

He *really could have* killed me, shot both my daughter and me. My son told me he carried a gun. I believed that person was trying to lure my daughter into the hallway or to push into my place. He knew my son had been arrested but what he didn't know is that I was home at that time. I still believe that today.

After that, people in the neighborhood really started calling me crazy but whatever worked to keep people from away from us, that is what I did.

Including being the Crazy, Angry Lady with the Four Kids.

*****

A new apartment, work, back to school. On the outside, everything seemed to be normal. However, that was far from the truth. The years went by and still utter chaos.

Visits from the police and children services were frequent. The two older children were not just teenagers, they were teens diagnosed, suffering with PTSD and refusing to go to therapy. The little ones weren't so little anymore and looking back, I had to be out of my mind to have survived that madness.

I am surprised that I didn't have a nervous breakdown. It was extremely difficult to stop replaying what had happened. It was like a bad movie that I couldn't take my eyes off of and I was mentally exhausted from it all. Everything reminded me of the horror. Things like the smell of coffee and bleach. I hated the color blue and owned nothing blue. I wanted to peel my skin off anytime someone touched me. Back then, I fell into the habit of throwing away clothes. If I had "one of those days", I would discard the entire outfit. Shoes and purse included. I was obsessed with cleanliness to the point that I often exhausted myself from staying up all night cleaning and rearranging furniture throughout the apartment. When I went to the laundry, I would pour extra gallons of water in the rinse cycle just to make certain that they were clean and at night I would get up several times to make sure that the door was locked and that the gates on the windows were secured.

    I avoided anywhere that I had suffered any abuse by anyone.

    Everywhere I look, there was a fight. The two older ones fighting each other then turning on me.

    Physical fighting and sometimes with weapons.

    A fight with the neighbor because her daughter threw water on mine. A fight, several fights with the schools that my children attended. A fight on the train after a woman pushed my baby as she went to sit down.

    A lot of physical violence in the home. It was a mess. The state sanctioned definition of domestic violence. Really just a lot of family violence.

    It had followed us.

    And it stayed a very long time resulting in chaos and confusion, incarceration, run aways, self-mutilation, truancy, substance abuse use, gang banging, teen pregnancy, school drop-out, family court and criminal court, sleepless nights, days looking for missing kids, psych hospital visits. The yelling, screaming, slamming doors and children disappearing for days. I was always accused of taking sides when trying to stop a fight. So, I devised a way to resolved that. It wasn't ideal but it worked,

And me in the streets trying to find them before something happened to them.

The joke was on me.

Something had already happened long before we got to that apartment.

Yeah there were some nice civilized moments, but they were so few and far in between that they were almost nonexistent.

They were good kids with a bad case of trauma.

I loved them still and through all the chaos and the ugliness, I never let them go. I was not going to give up on them.

I almost did.

Back then I did not know exactly why they did the things they did and why they were mean to me. Until I did.

For a long time, it was difficult to live with the guilt of all that they had been through. They missed out on so much because I made a decision that almost caused me my life and had just about costed them their childhood.

All of these years later, there are still 'those" moments and although they, we were not out of the woods yet, we have begun the long walk out of the forest.

Five years later, they were still in turmoil.

Eventually we became a little better while we continued to struggle with each other. It wasn't easy since we all were a reminder to each other of all that was. Of that life where it wasn't a life and even after leaving, there was still violence. It was crazy!!

We really didn't know how to love each other through the chaos and I think just tolerated one another while being the best family that we could. The craziness coupled with some moments of sanity, slowly, very slowly began to make things less crazy. For a moment any way. We slowly worked the holidays back into our life and THAT was no easy feat.

I believed that because my children were exposed to the world of extra curricula activities while living in the chaos, they had a point of reference as to what positive looked like. The afterschool programs, summer camps, sleep away camp, and even participating in school plays create a data base of memories that they were able to draw upon and laugh at.

Yes, laugh at.

I believe them seeing me and visiting me at work made a difference as well. Wherever that may have been. Every place I have ever worked, my children came by or visited or *created drama*. I wanted them to know what I did all day while I was at work, while they were at school.

It was important that they understand the concept of employment and what it looked like. Even that was chaotic and often I found myself embarrassed by what they would do or say.

When I returned to school, I made it a point to talk about my classes to them and for them to see me studying.

They also visited me at college. All of this was my way of helping them grow and heal and see that the violence that we lived in was not the only way to live. Things were still very, very chaotic but they were improving. *I think.*

18

AN INTERVENTION

As I WAITED FOR THE DIVORCE drama to play itself out, I tried as much as possible to live a normal life, whatever that was. But I guess, I wasn't trying hard enough.

*****

I was summoned to his office.

"Mrs. Norwood, I need to speak about your behavior. You cannot come to work like you have been."

What he was referring to is the fact that I had been showing up to work and somewhere during the school day I would begin to cry. It happened on multiple occasions and I was so caught up in my pain didn't realize that anyone noticed.

"You don't understand. My teenage children are out of control and I am stressed out because of my husband is stalking me."

He looked at me then got up and walked over to the door and closed it. Once he sat back down in his seat, he sighed then began talking.

"I understand more than you think I do. This is my ideal job. This is the job I worked my butt off to get but every day at the end of the day, I hate to go home. I have a sixteen-year old who is totally incorrigible. When I walk through these doors each morning, I come as the principal of this school and not as my daughters' father. It is the only way that I can do my job."

He commenced to describing my daughter in his home. I was shocked! Totally dumbstruck! He had to be lying!! I couldn't believe that a principal would be having almost the same problems with his teenage daughter that I was having. I mean he didn't exhibit *any* signs at all. Always in a suit and tie. Always visible throughout the school building, speaking with the students and staff. He didn't break a sweat, how was it possible that he could be having issues with his child? He was a principal of a school.

He then said this, *"You are a good worker and the students like you, but my priority is to the students and not you. You have to figure out how to work without your personal life creating havoc at work. I cannot tell you how to do that. I will suggest that you call out tomorrow, take a mental health day and figure it out."*

I took two days off. I thought about what he said, "*When I walk through these doors each morning, I come as the Principal and not my daughters' father"*.

I returned back to work two days later with a game plan. I figured that if it worked for him, it should work for me.

Each morning, prior to entering the school, I stood in front of the entrance doors and told 'Doreen' that she would have to wait for me outside, that I would be back for her at three o'clock. I did this for about six months and at the end of each work day I would walk out of that door and stop and say, "Ok Doreen, I'm back, let's go home" and in that moment, I would feel as if the weight of the world was just placed on my shoulder. I would become depressed and frankly, did not want to go home. Several times during the six months, I got caught by students leaving' Doreen' so some of the students started saying that I was crazy. I didn't care.

I was too busy trying to keep my job.

Eventually, I was able to walk straight inside of that building and get my work done.

Reflecting back, I am grateful for what I would like to refer to as an intervention. That principal didn't just save my job. He did not have to have that conversation with me. I am so grateful that he did. It helped me figure out how to compartmentalize, how to separate the pain of the past from my present situation leading me to start to heal. It helped me realize that I was not the only parent experiencing the teen age woes.

At that time, I was unable to grasp the significance of that conversation.

I transferred out the next school year.

Had to keep moving....

19

BY DEFAULT

WE WERE LEGALLY MARRIED IN MAY of 1990 and legally divorced in February of 2001.
February 14th to be exact. Valentine's Day.
That is the date that the divorce decree was certified by the Manhattan Supreme Court.

*****

I was tired of waiting and playing his game. He had refused to sign it a year ago and the judge said that I had to wait and another year went by. This particular day in February, once again, I had gone to the court to check on the status and this time the clerk came back and directed me to another window.

"Why are you sending me over there?," I asked.

"You have to sign it and I have to stamp it in order for it to be certified then you can have your copy."

"Excuse me?, not quite believing what he was saying,
"Are you saying that he signed it?"

"No. You were granted a judgement by Default. Once I put the court seal on it, it will be certified and you will be divorced on the grounds of Cruel and Inhuman Treatment."

When it was finished, I thanked him and exiting the room I just could not contain myself and began singing and skipping through the hall until I was stopped by a court officer instructing me to stop.

"My apologies Sir. I just received my divorce decree!"

He smiled and walked away.

I carried that document with me *every da*y for the next six years. I only asked the court for one thing: to be able to change my name back to Lesane.

He was ordered to pay child support but never did. Not until she was twenty. I didn't care. I wanted no ties. Nothing.

Just to no longer be attached to him legally.

I got that and that was the best Valentine's Day present ever. Yes. Ever in my life.

That marriage was actually nullified and voided the moment he struck me the first time. But I didn't know that back then. I was taught that marriage is forever and for better or worse. The only thing worse that could have happened is that he would have killed me.

It is only by the grace, the grace, the grace of God that I sit here today with minimal physical scars and no traumatic brain injury. My face was always the first place he struck.

I will never forget the first time he assaulted me.

It was an ambushed.

I was in the kitchen and heard him calling my name. As I walked out of the kitchen, he smashed me in the face with a telephone and broke the bridge of my nose. The imprint from the back of the phone travelled from my forehead down across my lips and ended just on top of my chin. As I sit here and write this, I can clearly remember what he said afterwards,

"Do you see what you made me do."

I was in shock and couldn't quite understand what happened. I tried to put together *what did I do*. Let me see, I thought to myself, I remembered being in the kitchen and hearing him call me and asked him to wait a minute. As I exited the kitchen to see what he wanted, he smashed me in the face with that telephone.

I started crying and the kids started crying and he began telling us to shut up and ran the kids into the back where the bedrooms were. That was one of maybe two things that he had done that he ever apologized to me for doing. Then he walked out of the apartment and left me standing there with my face bruised and bloody and all I could think about was that I had no phone.

Suppose there was an emergency, how would I call for help, not realizing that I needed help and medical attention. I ended up getting neither.

I asked Diane to watch my kids and walked over to his mother, home to tell her what he had done and that I wanted out.

Her response was " Ya'll young girls so quick to want to leave instead of trying to work it out".

I went back, retrieved my kids and that was that.

I really didn't know what else to do, how to respond. Nothing else was said about it. Until now.

What I didn't know back then but became clear to me much later is that he was a serial abuser. I was not the only "young girl" who wanted out. I was not the only one that he had abused nor would I be the last.

Nor would my children be the only children exposed to and traumatized by his actions. For me the most tragic part is that his mother and sisters knew this and said nothing.

In fact, that marriage exposed me to be verbally abused by one of his sisters.

*****

Working with women who have been abused, there is a commonality that I discovered quite by accident. When touching upon their family dynamics and interactions with their abusers' families, I hear that often there is another abuser to the victim. A family member.

While that person may not physically abuse them, the verbal abuse is just as damaging.

Words. Have. Power,

Abusers often get away with their actions because they are supported by their families who look and pretend not to see it, know about it but don't intervene, don't believe the victim, condones it and even supports the abuser over the victim. That is exactly what happened to me.

These are accounts that I have heard about many over the years.

I too have witnessed it and I have experienced it.

Divorce from the abuser also means divorce from the abusers' enablers, in my case anyway.

And it felt wonderful to free from them all.

Just marvelous!

*****

I am forever indebted to the law firm that handled my divorce. Pro Bono.

A year after I left, I was asked to attend a group for survivors and when I arrived, all of the women in attendance were given the opportunity for this law firm to assist us with getting divorced from our abusive husbands. I don't know who gave them my information. I am so glad that they did.

All we, I had to do was attend the next eight meetings and be available to meet with the attorney assigned. Eight months seemed like a long time but for me what was eight months compared to the now going on nine years.

I don't remember how many completed the process. I know that I did.

There was a difficult part and a frustrating part to all of it. Difficult because in order for the petition to be filed, I had to write out the incidents and dates of the abuse and the court would only consider a certain time period.

I clearly remember *not wanting to remember* and not wanting to write down any of those incidents because it had only been a year since I escaped that madness and I did not want to look back. But it was part of the work. Part of being free legally.

As I begin to write, I noticed that I wasn't hurting emotionally. I was more angry at what had happened to me. I was supposed to write up, I think, incidences from the past six months but no further than three years back.

I was able to list the abuse back to eight years.

I still have the original petition.

Now this law firm was helping me with no judgement and no expectation other than to help me become legally untangled. It all felt new and strange because here are these people who knows nothing about me but want to help me. Someone honestly wanted to help me. Us. This became another moment of shifting from the past hurts and disappointments to wow…*there are people out here who care.*

For the next two years, this attorney stuck by my side, kept me abreast to what was happening, never made me feel like she didn't care. She always, always, listen to what I had to say, addressed my concerns, and reassured me that she understood how frustrating the process was but that she would help get me through.

And she did.

What was so frustrating is that it took two years because he refused to sign it. He had the nerves to refuse to sign it. During this time, he was trying to see his daughter but I knew that was just a ploy to find out where I was. This attorney helped me to make sure that it didn't happen.

Long after the group ended and until the divorce decree was certified and served to him, she, they honored their word and I will forever be grateful.

With all of that said and done, the sun shone really brightly that day, February 14, 2001 right there in the courthouse in lower Manhattan.

I was free! Free! Of him. His mother and his sister.

All I thought about is how I would be celebrating.

My celebration started the very next morning at the Social Security Administration.

Changed my last name back to Lesane.

From one place to the next I went with that newly minted Divorce Decree and changed, removed that name identifying or tying me to that person.

Unfortunately, I was not able to change my undergraduate degree but that is okay. It doesn't negate the fact that it is mine.

It was exhilarating yet I cried a lot at night because I really thought that it was a dream, that I would wake up and find that the divorce was just a cruel joke being played on me.

I was afraid that I would lose the Decree so I carried it around for six years. It was my security blanket. I felt safe being able to touch it wherever, whenever.

Although I was running around as fast as the days would break to remove his surname from my documents, in the back of my mind I couldn't process that it was really over.

I started wearing one of those paper name tags that people where at conferences or events and for the people who continued to call me by his last name, I would not even respond to them. At all. Didn't matter that we worked together. Didn't matter where we met. If you knew me by his last name and referred to me as such once the divorce was final, I would not respond.

While I was going through this state of euphoria because I was finally physically and legally free from this person, I had absolutely no idea that mentally and emotionally, I was still his prisoner and still in victim mode.

What the Order of Protection could not do and did not do, the Divorce Decree did. It freed me to be safe. It freed me physically and psychologically. I was no longer bound to that man or his family. In my mind, I was free and I was safe.

Only I wasn't free.

I still was in survival mode and had no clue how deeply entrenched I really was. I had no idea of the mental, emotional and psychological damage that my babies and I sustained.

That the reality, my reality is that although I was no longer bound to him, it didn't make any of the internal wounds go away. It didn't solve any of the problems that the abuse created. Escaping and getting divorced only freed me physically.

Emotionally and psychologically I was a mess.

A hot unmitigated mess.

20

FOR NOW

As time went on, two years went by, then turned into five years. It was about this time, now divorced from him that people were asking "when are you going to get married again. *Me? Marry again?*

I was beyond a hot mess. I was scared and hurting and just couldn't find my way out of the pain. My choices of men weren't the best. I needed to take care of me. I just did not know how.

During those years, I was trying to transition out of the school system and began working part time for a specific agency. The guys there were cruel. When it became obvious that I wasn't going to date anyone there, they began harassing me and calling me Ice Queen, the Mute, Stuck Up, and if I had a dollar for every time one of them called me 'that light skinned bitch.' I'd been rich. After about four months, I resigned. Just couldn't deal with it anymore.

I didn't want to.

Over the years, my path crossed with a couple of them and although I was cordial, it was difficult engaging in conversation. You know, pretending that it was nice to see them was no easy feat. One even asked why didn't I talk to anyone and stated, *"No one liked you because you acted like you were better than everyone else. You know,* he said, *like you were too good."*

No. I told him. I had just left my then husband and was running for my life and was caught up in my own pain and my issues at that time were far too great to be hanging out and dating. Besides I don't mix work with my personal. He looked at me and asked why didn't I say anything to anyone and I told him quite honestly it was no one's business.

Today, I am glad that the two possible men that I found myself attracted to didn't work out. I didn't know at the time but neither would have been good for me.

One I met as I was trying to get divorced. We never even held hands or hugged. I was not at the stage that I wanted to be touched. Not even hugs from my own children. I was struggling with my past and battling what I was feeling for that man. I couldn't quite put my finger on it but there was something that kept me away from him although I was crazy about him. As I stood at a distant clutching my heart, I was able to see beyond what I was feeling and see that he was a womanizer with multiple children by multiple women. I had dodged a bullet. There were some things I discovered about him that wasn't good. Things that were no good for me or my kids.

I did end up dating a couple of guys but it never worked out. My drama plus their drama, both was just too much drama for me.

As I began my journey to find out why did I seem to always find myself with a guy that wasn't any good for me, I also struggled to stay away from dating but because I didn't want to be alone I drifted back into the tornado.

My own personal cycle of abuse was like this: I would do some work on myself and then date, usually for two years or so, then I would wake up one morning and realize that I was being abused. Being manipulated and lied to and cheated on, to me, is not only unhealthy but emotional abuse. Emotionally abuse is very painful, almost as painful as being physically abused. I would then stop dating for another two years or so, work on myself, therapy, school, not quite back in church yet then back to dating.

I was still just surviving.

The truth be told, this part of my life explains how easy it was to become involved with the wrong man and eventually I did and what really snapped me out of this cycle of abuse is a man that *I thought* we were dating for four years. I always thought we were a couple but there was no we. I believed him and in him.

I saw all the Red Flags and ignored them all.

He was very good at his craft.

He was a Bread Crumber.

You don't know what a Bread Crumber is?

A Bread Crumber is a person who manipulates a person emotionally by feeding them bits and pieces of their time. You will always eat but will never be full. The goal of the Bread Crumber is to do just enough to keep their victim emotionally attached and emotionally invested. Spend some time here, disappear, spend some time there, "busy working" but enough phone contact to keep you "hungry", a week of full fledge attention, got to leave town for business, all the right words via text....first thing in the morning, "thinking of you".

All of the above.

Bread Crumbers are in all walks of life.

But in this case, it's about abuse in a relationship. Most call it leading a woman on. Or a man. I call it Bread Crumbing.

Just enough to keep the victim or victims, emotionally involved and emotionally invested in a *very non-existent relationship.*

Eventually I discovered that there were three of us.

Then two of them.

We went out one evening and I stayed over his place and awoke to hear him in the bathroom talking. It was three in the morning and as I crept up to the door, which was ajar, I heard him saying, *"Please don't be angry at me. I had a rough day at work and took a sleeping pill when I got in. I'm sorry I didn't hear the phone."*

I almost died right here. I had heard that line more than once. Twice. Honestly, many times over the four years.

I turned around from the door, got dressed and then pushed the bathroom door open wide and announced very loudly that I was leaving. He turned and dropped the phone and I ran out of his apartment, down six flights crying into the night. Unable to get a taxi, I began to walk home. Within ten minutes of leaving he began calling my phone.

I wouldn't answer.

All that I could think about is how stupid I was.

How could I not see it?

Why?

What was wrong with me?

What I didn't realize then is that there was nothing wrong with me. My decision to believe in him was based on the lies he told me and the fact that he misrepresented himself. I accept full responsibility for believing him and trusting in him. Still, his actions were a reflection of his character not mine.

About eighteen months went by before I ran into that man again. I spotted him on the opposite side of the train car I entered it and turned away. A few minutes later I heard him call my name. I turned, smiled, nodded my head and continued my conversation on my phone. Several years later, he sent me an email saying that he saw my profile on LinkedIn. He wanted to congratulate me on the work that I was doing with abused women. He didn't apologize for treating me badly but did want me to know that he was hurt that I had stop speaking to him.

I chalked that up to a teachable moment by not responding to that email. It had Door to Abuse written all on it and I was not about to step through that door again. Not me.

Back to the drawing board. But this time was different. That event changed my perspective on many things. It was through this experience that my personal cycle of abuse ended.

I was learning to walk away. *I walked away.*

I was done with that and was even better when everyone finally stopped asking when was I going to remarry.

After another try or two at dating, with one informing me that he doesn't usually date smart girls because they think they know everything.

What? Seriously? Being free to read and engage in good conversation is very much who I am, me doing so is non- negotiable. Subsequently, I chose not to date and to keep my standards so high that those who are up to no good will keep it moving and not even try me.

In all fairness, I was not in the position to be dating anyone. Not the ones who meant me well and who genuinely cared for me or the ones who had their own issues that needed tending to.

Besides, I was discovering that I liked being alone.

*****

Once the healing process began and I began the journey upward and forward, it had become too late. The standards I set for myself was far beyond what any man could grasp and I refused to lower them *or* to inflict them upon anyone. Relationships requires a lot of work and then there are the rough patches. That is not something I wanted to deal with and not a burden that I would place on a man.

I am not in the business of mistreating people and was now at the place where I was not going to allow anyone to mistreat me.

My unintentionally crafted solitude left me with the blissful consequence of being single and the perfect way to learn love me and to be the best person possible that I could be with me

My constructed solitude became a welcomed peace.

My journey back to life came with a steep price but *for me* it was well worth it.

And I was leaving Survival mode.

21

AMEN

It saddens me that the church hasn't been more responsive to the needs of women and children who are living with violent men. While there are houses of faith that are responsive, they are few and far in between.

Like society, or the world as the church refers to society, the victim continues to be blamed and then shamed into staying. Just like many of the other manipulative tactics that abusers used to control their victims, unfortunately the Bible is also used as a way of victim shaming and victim blaming and compelling the abused to remain with their abuser.

They are fed scripture, prayed over, condemned for not being submissive to their husbands, then sent back to be beaten as if it is the will of God. Not so, the Bible is very clear on domestic violence. It does not condone it or family violence in any way and even speaks against verbal abuse.

*****

How ostracized we were sitting there in that back pew beaten, battered and bruised and no one said a word to me or my children. I sat there dressed in my Sunday finest often with a pair of shades to cover the black eyes yet unable to cover the swollen and busted lip or the lumps on my forehead. Still no one offered a kind word or any word. Every single Sunday month after month and year after year, we attended and it was like being in the church with no one else there.

Like being ex communicated.

The grown-ups ignored me and the children teased my children. I had long been asked to stop teaching in the children Sunday school by the time the taunts towards my two older children began, *"Your father beats your mother"*.

They went from being included to being excluded. They went from actively participating in the activities to straight up being ignored. There was nothing that I could do or say since the in laws attended the same church. Sat right there in the front pew every Sunday as if nothing was wrong.

I will not say that I felt abandoned by God because I did not. What I felt was nothing. *Absolutely nothing.*

I can't say and I won't say that He allowed me to be abused.

I didn't know Him back then.

My idea of who He was, was based on being dragged from the Bronx to Brooklyn each weekend to a different church as a child. I didn't really hear the sermons that were preached because I didn't understand why people were falling out in the aisles.

I didn't understand why my mother was sending money to the man on television in exchanged for a small red piece of cloth that had absolutely no power. It didn't change or improve the conditions of that environment. He got richer and we stayed poor and broken. I didn't understand the whole reading the Bible, her reading the Bible each morning then comparing everything that happened to the devil.

You see, my idea of who God was developed from a place of fear and confusion and that same fear and confusion kept me glued to a man that was severely abusing me under the pretense of wives are to submit to their husbands, to divorce is a sin and til death do us part.

Imagine how rich I would be if I had a dollar for every time I heard, what God put together let no man throw asunder. Talk about spiritual abuse.

It was rampant and came from all sides. My mother, his mother and the church.

It was real and at this point, I was only going to church because I was conditioned to go. I had no point of reference other than what I was shown. Nothing was explained.

So the thought to question or blame God never entered my mind. I was dead on the inside and almost dead on the outside. Hopeless and helpless.

Yet I stayed. In church.

I stayed until one Sunday I approached the reverend and told him (although the entire church knew what was going on). He responded by standing there and looking at me and after about three minutes he said, *"You should be glad that he married you since you already had kids"*.

I left that Sunday and never went back. Not to that church or any for over eight years.

*****

I awoke one Sunday morning many years later and just knew that the time had come. I knew that I had to get back into church but this time it would be different. I was not going to a church that someone invited me to or that I had visited with anyone. The search took almost a year.

From one house of worship to the next and for those who call it church hoping, so be it. For me it was more personal than ever, my soul knew what it needed and where it needed to be. It was no longer about other people opinion or where people wanted me to be or do. I was in the fight of my life *for my life* and my needs outweighed people opinions.

Eventually twelve, thirteen churches later, I walked into one and my very soul felt as if the seat I sat in was reserved for me. There were things going on there too, but I was different. It wasn't about the people or the pastor or the program.

It was about me and having my eyes on the Cross and not the pulpit. It was there that my very life began to change. I cursed less. I smiled more. As I learned more about who God is, my faith increased, I began to feel less afraid, less alone, more confident about life and about me. I didn't want to fight if someone bumped into me.

Felt less stressed, less angry.

I was starting to feel alive.

I still struggled with trust issues but after a year there began to speak to the parishioners.

For the next three years, I sat and was replenished and restored and yes, redeemed. It was during this time that the calling that God place on my life was revealed.

It was during a Friday night service that I receive my task. The pastor came out and began speaking "*You are running from the very thing that you were prepared to do and that although what had happened to you seemed unfair, it was to prepare you for others who are currently enduring*". After he said those words, he then said, *"I don't know why I said that or who it's for but now it's time to worship.* It seemed as though he was speaking directly to me.

The revelation was so surreal as I was being pressed by someone to facilitate a domestic violence group and I kept saying no. Until three weeks later, on a Friday night, at church, it happened again. The pastor came out and it seemed as if only he and I was in that sanctuary. He up front on the pulpit and me all the way in the back sitting in the last of twenty-five rows.

He said, *"You went through something that was unfair to you and now you are being called to help those who are coming after you. I know that you don't want to do it but you, you have been prepared for a moment such as this."*

It was the one of most incredible yet life affirming thing that I had ever heard. It was as if he was speaking directly to me and it is then that I started to live and not just survive.

That night I surrendered to the fact that I was going to be doing something related to domestic violence.

I just didn't know what.

*****

Just as I was returning back, I was invited to an event that was being done for Recovery Month to speak about my experience with domestic violence. The event was held in the basement of a church in Harlem. I went and inadvertently disclosed that I as a child I lived in a household where drugs and alcohol was prevalent. I related it to how children who grow up in those types of living environments sometimes grow up to be involved in unhealthy relationships and that I was one of those children. Just all grown up.

What I didn't know is that the Senior pastor of this church, Memorial Baptist Church, was sitting in the audience listening. After I finish speaking she invited me to speak at Sunday service about being a survivor of domestic violence. I accepted her invitation and that very next day, I stood for the first time on a pulpit during Sunday morning service speaking to a church congregation about domestic violence. Since then I have had the distinct honor of repeating that on many occasions in a variety of houses of worship and have had the opportunity to speak on several occasions to a group of members at a couple of organized events through the church.

While there are still too many houses of worship that don't talk about it and don't want to hear about it, there are some that do or are willing to learn how to recognize and respond. I thank God for them

*****

My preparation was not yet done but was to continue across town at another church. Whether you believe it or not, God will move you whether you want to or not. I walked out of that house of worship one Friday night and the following Sunday morning walked into another church where once again, my only goal was to sit. My past experience forced me to become an Observer.
 For the first year, I worshipped, paid my tithes and went about my daily life.

During this time, I began to cross paths with people from my past. Some of them expressed amazement that I was even alive. Most were trying to figure out what happened to me, like *why was I smiling*. People began to tell me that I had change (and I told them they were crazy), but it was true.

People wanted to know how could I not be angry and bitter after all that had happened and still others, how could I forgive him after all of the abuse and humiliation that he put me through, *why would I forgive him.*

Because I had to, I said to anyone who asked. Not for him *but for me.*

For my sanity.

They couldn't figure out this new Doreen.

I couldn't figure her out either.

She was new to me too.

22

IT'S ABOUT TIME

I RETURNED TO COLLEGE FOR MY undergraduate in Business and that had a profound effect on my life in a weird way beyond the academics.

Being in school made me feel safe and well, alive. It wasn't the greatest of experience, but it gave me a sense of accomplishment and in it I was hoping to be a role model to my kids. To show them a different life.

Throughout that time, while I excelled academically and completed my studies, at home I still was a hot mess and so were my kids who were now turning into full fledge teenagers.

In hindsight, I didn't realize how much pain I was in and that my Type A personality was just a way of feeling like I had a sense of control in an environment that was very much out of control and out of order.

In 2002, I completed my undergraduate studies and several years later, resigned from working in the school system. I had outgrown that position.

While my transition into the non-profit sector was gradual and meticulously planned, it is there that I entered the professional world of substance abuse treatment, the criminal justice system and of all things, domestic violence.

In my mind, it was so unintentional but in the great scheme of things, it was the beginning of everything to come.

From a personal standpoint, I no longer thought about it. It was done and over. The divorce was finally finalized and I was free.

*****

My role at the first organization was initially part time and to re acclimate the clients to the education process During the intake process as I was asking scripted questions, many would share details of their life. The participants, were women newly released from upstate prison or part of the Alternate To Incarceration (ATI) program out of either Rikers Island or Brooklyn Treatment Court, who shared details of how they ended up incarcerated and their experience with abusive partners. When I shared this with my supervisor during supervision, she decided that she would have me facilitate a group for the women who disclosed either domestic violence. This group took on a life of its own and I was shocked at how many were abused prior to incarceration.

Formally and professionally, I knew nothing about domestic violence and really didn't think about my history.

During this time as I continued to do the academic component, I met someone who gave me some information on how it was possible for the women to attend college. After taking this information back to my supervisor, I was granted permission to create the CAP or College Awareness Program as a way of having these women see that education could open doors for them and give them a second chance at their dreams.

I wanted them to know that they were more that former felons and more than just a client. They were humans.

That got me in trouble with my colleagues who felt that because I had no prior experience working in the treatment field as they called it, I should stick to calling them what they were. Clients. I continued to refer to them as ladies.

About six months later, a cohort for this organization invited me to take a thirty-hour certification course for domestic violence and substance abuse. I did and toss the certification in a tote never expecting to ever use it. About three years later, I began job hunting again.

I was a runner and I did not stay anywhere too long. Just in case. I mean, I had no idea where he was or if he was still looking for me. I didn't know and wasn't planning on sticking around to find out.

*****

I landed at an environment where I was tasked with working with large groups of adults, sometimes up to seventy-five persons with multiple barriers and yes, multi personalities. The site was located not too far from Covenant House. It was here that I met a co-worker who helped me get the therapeutic assistance that I needed to cope from a place of normalcy. If it wasn't for this person, I probably would have lost everything including my mind.

What I didn't know is that I was being prepared to speak before large groups of people with diverse perspectives and from diverse walks of life. It was an interesting place with interesting coworkers. Here, I was once again in trouble for calling the clients ladies and gentlemen instead of referring to them as Clients.

I remembered how I felt being a Client. How cold and clinical and disconnected by the service provider I felt. Almost as if I wasn't worthy of their time and on several occasions, have had some say that 'all of you clients are the same'.

So, no. I do not refer to anyone as a client. And when I do, it's lightly and respectfully. They may be a client at an agency or organization but to me they are more and deserve to be treated with dignity and respect as a person regardless of what the need may be.

Two things happened at this job. One, during the screening process domestic violence kept coming up. *Again and again.* It seems that everywhere I turned or found myself, someone wanted to tell me about their experience with being abused. Many sat crying in my cubicle, not wanting to return back to the home that awaited them at the end of the day.

I did not know how to help them. I was still learning how to help myself.

I would be lying if I said that I had it all together and that life was great. That was still years away in the future. Yes, I had a good job, my kids were okay and on the outside, I was an excellent worker and a sharp dresser, but on the inside, there was a lot of turmoil.

I was getting better but still had my days.

There I also met a person that I will call CJ. One day I happened to walk up on him as he was saying some really derogatory things to the residents of Covenant House. I became highly offended and he was like,

"Please Ms. Doreen, you don't know nothing about this. They're just runaways who need to take their asses back home instead of hanging in the streets."

"*Really?*" I said, *You don't know their story or what brought them to Covenant House.*"

"*They're just juvies who don't want to follow the rules at home that's all,* he replied. *Why are you defending them? Look at them and look at you.*", he said.

"*Yeah, look at me. Take a good look because I use to be one of them!!* " I said angrily.

"*What!! Stop lying!*", *I mean, what!*" He exclaimed and proceeded to call me a liar and tell me to stop rooting for the underdogs because it was a waste of time.

Subsequently, I told him my story of how I ended up at Covenant House then as an abused wife. He tried to prompt me to tell my story and I refused. He kept saying that it would benefit those lost kids in Covenant House as he called them. Still I refused. Especially since I had not ever, *ever* talked about being in Covenant House or what happened to me while I was there.

And at that point, as far as I was concerned, who wanted to hear about domestic violence? I didn't. I had survived and moved on with my life. I wanted no parts of that and besides who wanted to hear my story of beatings, rapes and darkness.

I had started going back to church, a different one, and again, no one knew my name which was perfect. I sat in the back in the last pew on the end of the row. I worshipped, paid my tithes and left. I did not join or attend any functions.

*****

From a professional standpoint, it was just beginning. The time had come. Focused and Intentionality had settled in and the more centered I became, the more I understood my purpose, the more intentional I became. I began to seriously think about what CJ said about doing a domestic violence workshop at Covenant House.

After considering all of my options and thinking about what that pastor said about being prepared for a moment such as this, I decided to take a chance.

It became all about branding myself as a credible and reputable Domestic Violence Educator. I figured that since I have a background in education and creating curricula, it wouldn't be that hard and I began to design customized power points on different themes of domestic violence. *Domestic Violence 101: Facts Vs. Myths; Parenting and Domestic Violence* were my first two. I have since created over seventeen more including *Domestic Violence: What It Is Not.)*

I started volunteering to facilitate workshops on domestic violence and went back to Covenant House to do exactly that. It was my first gig and where I cut my teeth on my way to becoming who I am now. How ironic that my journey landed me right back to one of the places I started out at.

I began research on how to become a public speaker and in 2010 stumbled upon the book, *The Brand Within* by Daymond John. You know *FUBU* and now *Shark Tank*. I read the book cover to cover highlighting in yellow what stood out to me and then the second reading highlighted in pink. It was my go to book. This book became my new divorce papers. I carried it everywhere and pulled it out anywhere. It was The Manual. This book helped me create *and* sustain my brand, Sunshine In My Living Room and get paid to do so.

My first paid gig was for the New York City Public Library. Only three people showed up.

THRIVER: My Story To Tell

Telling my story came much later.

23

NAKED

ALTHOUGH MANY YEARS HAD GONE BY since I had escaped and the divorce was finalized, it wasn't until people started asking me to tell my story that it became evident to me how damaging intimate partner violence is long term. Looking back, I didn't realize what I was being asked to do would affect me so badly but also change the course of my life.

*****

There was a nakedness that happened when I first started telling *my story*. I could facilitate a workshop on the topic with no problem. Being personal about the information was another story. Immediately after I would finish speaking, I would feel like I had just been stripped of my clothes and that everyone was staring at me, laughing and judging me for staying. I would find myself transported back into those moments with my former abuser calling me "Stupid" and how nobody cared about me. His words seemed to ring true even all of those years later.

Especially when you tried to engage someone in a conversation and they would appear not to be interested. They would all say how sorry that they are that you went through all of that then walk off, or they would tell you how great you were standing up there telling your story then excuse themselves and walk away.

While disclosure with a trained professional is one thing, it is entirely another when doing so publicly.

Standing there afterwards just stripped naked for a bunch of strangers who only came to say that they participated in a domestic violence event really destroyed any feelings of accomplishments and awoke all of the emotions that I had worked so hard to forget.

Still operating from a place of trauma.

I went from being abused by my former spouse to *feeling abused*, exposed and taken advantage of by others whose only motives were to benefit themselves by having a victim show up and tell their story at some event designed to look like they were really engaged with survivors; it set me back emotionally. These events where everyone always say that they are honoring the victims yet always placed the victim or survivor *at the end* of the program or event to speak or share their story (testimony) Always.

The guest(s) of Honor *last*…..

Only at domestic violence events.

You see, being a former survivor of intimate partner violence opens up the flood gates to be used by people.

More often than not after the event is over, the victim/survivor is sent on their not so merry way to sit in all those emotions that were dredged up and the person who asked them to "tell their story" is nowhere to be found.

There are no follow up phone calls to check in on you.

No aftercare for the wounds that have been savagely ripped open. No debriefing.

There are no offers for after care counseling to make sure you are alright.

The person who constantly called to make certain you would be there suddenly becomes unreachable via email, phone or text and while that is the nature of the business, it further destroys the person who was invited to 3edtell their horrible story. There is usually no consideration of this person, the victim, survivor afterwards.

None.

Part of the nakedness is a vulnerability that is easily exploited. That exploitation comes from the survivors' wanting and *needing* to be included and accepted.

To feel wanted and loved.

Instead you are left feeling revictimized and is re traumatized. You're left feeling used and discarded.

It is how I once felt.

I experienced it more times than I really care to remember when I initially found myself "in demand" to tell my story and it comes from a place of having to learn how to trust again and at times, *trusting the wrong people.*

For me, I did not trust anyone and that made re building my life difficult as I started venturing out into the world trusting again. *I didn't know how.* Unhealed people often do not make the most rational decisions.

Unfortunately, I ended up swinging too far over and trusted everyone and needless to say, many that I came in contact with, did not deserve my trust, time or respect.

It was so easy to be manipulated and feel like you are actually a part of something until you realize that you are not. The callousness and the dis interest by those in attendance had a way forcing me to retreat back into my pain and my shame.

I felt naked and ashamed as if I said something wrong or offensive. I remember on several occasions, I vomited afterwards. On other occasions I would rush out of the venue and head home avoiding any contact with anyone.

The nakedness was overwhelming and was often replaced with feeling invisible. It would be many, many years before I would become strong enough to let go of the feeling. It was really by trial and error that it happened and learning to say No.

*****

There is a human cost when engaging people who have been traumatized. Really, there is. Over the past nine plus years as an advocate and as a clinician, I have heard this many times over from those who have been abused first by their partners then by others.

Working with women who have participated in domestic violence events share this with me.

How naked and exposed they feel afterwards.

Or how "stupid" they felt sitting around just to be called as the event is almost over, some stating that they never even got the opportunity to speak. Left feel used and dejected but continuing to go along so that you don't hurt anyone feelings even though yours are.

I had become so angry after one event, I made a decision that I would *no longer let others decide how I would tell my story.*

I needed to take control of my life that was still out of control from the many years of abuse. After all, it was *my life and my story*. Only after I decided to do so, was I able to move pass that feeling of being used and naked and begin to focus on what was truly important: the message that my story was delivering for someone in that audience.

The person who had invited me wasn't happy and even told me that I never would be invited back. She never did or any of her colleagues. After all, as far as they were concerned, *I was just another victim and* could easily be replaced. That's what she said.

Talk about Power and control!

That was okay. I was beginning to get stronger on the inside and it was only after that event that the feeling of being naked never happened or haunted me again.

24

PROCESSING

BEING CALM WAS EXTREMELY DIFFICULT. NOT only that, I was an emotional wreck running on highs and lows. I was easily frustrated and lost my temper quickly and often. I really didn't cry back then, not because I couldn't or anything like that, I just didn't. I was too busy in self protect mode.

My decision making process was actually, for many years, based on my emotions and I had to learn how to not to be guided by how I felt.

I trusted no one and didn't want to be around anyone. It was now my responsibility to protect me. I lived in a total state of hyper vigilance where I thought everyone was the enemy and had resorted to changing my routine every three days to keep anyone from knowing where I was, where I went, how I got into the neighborhood or what time. Just anything that would prevent anyone from knowing my schedule.

It was so bad that I would leave the lights on in my apartment so that no one knew when I was home or not at home. I also continued to isolate myself.

What changed during this time is that the same wall that I had built to keep people out is the same wall I used to include people, *but at a distance*, as I began to heal.

A door was added to the wall so that I wasn't trapped behind it. It also gave me the power to choose who and how close any given person could come into my personal space.

Boundaries are very important for living a healthy life personally, professionally and in my case, also spiritually. I knew nothing about boundaries.

It was one of the most trying things I had to learn.

In relationships where there is abuse, there are no boundaries because of the one-sided power play that is in effect and attempting to take a stance can create more harm than good. This also applies to victim blaming statements. The accuser over steps their boundaries by assuming that they know what is best for the victim which steals the victims voice and further disempowers the abused person.

I mean, I could hear me speaking, why didn't anyone else? *What made their voice more important than mine?* There was just so much happening at one time. I was trying to live and raise my children as best as I possible could *and get well emotionally at the same time.*

*****

While most people including the professionals are just starting to understand that escaping is not the end but in actuality the beginning, they fail to take into account the toll the beatings take on the body, the soul and the spirit of the abused.

You see, a person is made up of body, soul and spirit.

I am.

Their body is their connection to the physical world through the five senses.

My body is my connection to the physical world. Sight, hearing, taste, touch and smell. Each is negatively affected due to the abuse.

The soul gives us our personality and lives out our relationship with God, others and self and is comprised of the mind both conscious and unconscious, the will and emotions, all which are impacted by the abuse whether it is physical or psychological.

The Spirit is the part that gives us meaning and purpose in life and at the deepest level, it enables us to love God, others and self.

But when the body is beaten and sexually violated, and when the soul and spirit is crushed by manipulation and intimidation or accusations and condemnation of liking the unhealthy situation and judged for remaining there, the person fails to thrive and the despair and hopelessness sets in leaving those that are being abused depressed, hopeless and unable to see a future without the abuse.

When the body is battered, it affects the soul and the spirit.

When the soul is crushed it affects the spirit and the body.

It is HERE that victims lose hope.

It is here that I lost hope.

When one is affected all three are affected.

One is never separate from the other.

I couldn't separate them.

THRIVER: My Story To Tell

On the outside I was well put together and very efficient at work. On the inside that was another story and exactly what I was: *Crushed. To. My. Very Soul. Spiritually depleted from the physical and verbal beatings and yes, the lack of empathy, compassion.....love.*

There is nothing more hopeless or helpless than a person who has been crushed to their soul, the very essence of who they are. It is here that the blackness of the abuse has settled in and it is where I became engulfed in grief and despair until my spirit was restored.

*****

I didn't watch shows that had violence. I couldn't and we didn't celebrate anything. We didn't know how to. The traumatic memories cut so deep that holidays ceased to exist as a way of us coping with them. Whether it was anniversaries birthdays or holidays we steered clear of them and just went through those days as if they were just another day on the calendar until one day my Baby Gurl hamster got killed by my sons' ferret. We had a funeral for it and while it was sad, we found humor in it and that opened the door for them to live again in the moment and not the past.

It wasn't perfect but it was a start.

It was not easy to get to this point or be here either.

After I did all that I possibly could to set my children on a path of healing, I began to focus on all of the things that would benefit me, strengthen me and make me a better person.

I wasn't just trying to become free from the past abuse but was also to parent myself in the process. I need to teach myself how to love me, how to take care of me, how to speak to me and what to listen to.

I wanted to show myself, that little Doreen, who grew up but was not raised that what happened wasn't her fault and as a child that she was just a victim of circumstances. I wanted her to know that everything she endured and survived was developing who I am. *Who I was to become.* She needed to know that her inner strength and endurance was what *I* needed to become all that I am. Her compassion and love for learning would set the course for my healing so far into the future that is now my present.

But in order for that to happen, she had to be a part of all that happened, she had to witness and feel the injustices that were never meant to destroy her but to grow her into the person who sits here today writing this story beyond surviving and not as a survivor but a Thriver.

I decided to take care of me the way I thought I should have been taken care of as a child and as I walked that course, it became evident to me that all that was endured and lived had to happened. It was never meant to kill me.

It was going to be gut wrenching, deep down, way back therapy and I had no choice but to pull out the shovel to dig up somethings and bury others.

The process was not going to be easy or pretty.

I fought, kicked, scratched and avoided looking at how my emotions and destructive behavioral patterns as they applied to me. *Until I couldn't any more.* It took years, yes, years for me to not react to things that brought back the memories, the triggers.

Learning how to move out of those moments was a job in and of itself.

Identifying them was not an easy task and learning to manage those emotions and stop operating from a place of trauma was so challenging. I began to realize that my disposition affected everyone I came in contact with, especially my children. I wanted to give up and go back to where I felt safe, *but wasn't.*

Another confession I have to make is really relative to survivors (not all) who abusers controlled the finances, prevented them from working or going to school to get a degree or trade.

I had no concept of managing finances. I had no idea what a credit score was until I walked into that furniture store hoping to get beds for my children after I escaped. Like many others who were in marriages, relationships rifted with abuse, finances were the last thing on my mind, with survival being first.

Learning how to manage my finances, understanding what a credit score was, understanding exactly what my 401k was and how it all was tied to my life was challenging. Even opening and maintaining a bank account was foreign. As important as they are, they were not important at that time.

Finding my way back was my priority and so for years, I continued to suffer because I was financially illiterate. Ironically, my BS was in Business Management and at that time I didn't connect that with what I was learning in college and how was relevant it was to my personal life.

Yes, things had gone from bad to ugly really quickly.

As a matter of fact, the only thing solved was the fact that I had escaped and the truth of the matter as much as that was a huge deal, it just wasn't enough.

Starting from scratch, from a blank page is exactly what had to happened in order to recover from it all. You start all over.

I started all over. I had to.

My sense of safety was totally destroyed, and I had to learned to tackle that feeling of always feeling unsafe and did so in various ways such as taking classes such as film production, yoga, dancing and swimming. Being in these classes helped me to be around people outside of work but it wasn't easy. In the back of my mind, he would one day show up to wherever I would be and so I continued to live on the edge and in flight mode.

I went to shows and museums to try and find my way back to in crowds. It was daunting and scary and I would deliberately stay in the shadows, by the exits, *just in case I had to escape.*

I also had to learn how to handle the very things that triggered those things that reminded me of the past abuse. It could be anything. A thought, memory, a smell, a song on the radio, a restaurant, an amusement park. There are two smells I can't. *I just couldn't take.*

Coffee and bleach.

Coffee reminded me of living in that household as a child and ALL of the horrible things that happened in that place. It has been over forty years and I have only drunk coffee three times in my life. Only because I didn't know how to say no. Today I don't and won't drink coffee. Now

I can smell it without thinking about those years. And the bleach. The Bleach and the blood.

It could be seeing violence or hearing an argument, or it could be something that someone did to me.

It could be a touch, a hug, the close proximity of a male.

Like the one who began to sexually harass me in a church that I was attending *and* the response from the powers that be. His inappropriate touching and unwanted advances sent me into an emotional tailspin. It took me back fifteen years and brought back the nightmares that had long ago stopped. I found myself crying on Saturday nights, torn between attending church in the morning or staying home.

It was extremely difficult to deal with it and reporting it turned into a nightmare. It dragged on for about nine months. I felt like I had done something wrong. *Maybe I should not have said anything.* Then I was told by the associate pastor that I needed to repent for being disobedient and causing division *for reporting it* (even though other people corroborated it). I was torn between staying and leaving. I was no longer safe there and removed myself. I walked away from that place and did not look back and went back into *Safety Planning mode.* Full force.

Almost seventeen years after escaping from my ex-spouse.

Once a situation occurs or an argument happens, I will leave and will not go back. Not because I don't want to be there but because I no longer feel safe. There are people that I miss dearly from many places. However, I no longer feel safe around them. While I am nineteen years removed from the abuse, there are still moments that if I feel attacked, I will disconnect myself from the person, people, business, situation and I won't go back.

Feeling safe is important to me. It is a priority.

Being in a safe space is important to me.

My desire to live became greater anything else and that compels me to walk away from anything and everything that served me no purpose.

Especially when it means compromising my safety or myself.

I did not care how I looked or what people thought about me and it was only when I began applying what I was learning that the real change began.

The practical application led to a mind shift and that helped me immensely.

It helped me and my children. I was learning to parent them from the present and not from a place of the past.
In that space I was learning to see others *and life* differently as well.

25

EMBRACING DEATH

EVER SINCE I WAS A CHILD, even hearing that someone died frightened me. The mere mention of it would bring nightmares and insomnia. The first funeral that I ever attended was that of my late father, then my aunt, my former father in law and then last year my mother.

There is something strangely beautiful about death. After being in that life or death situation and smelling it on myself, after almost being murdered, I was no longer afraid. I am no longer afraid. It was no longer cliché to me that "death is a part of life." It was fact. *It is a fact.*

Eventually Death also took on a whole new meaning to me. In order for me to live, all of the old had to die. The old fears, old habits, how I presented myself…you know from a place of pain mixed with anger or fear of rejection. I had to put to rest all emotional attachments that kept me rooted in the past and stuck in my own way.

In order to move forward there were people, places and things that needed to be buried. There was just no way that I could live without the death of certain things.

It wasn't easy to embrace this concept and as a matter of fact, I struggled with it for a while before I came to the conclusion that there was no other way.

This type of death led to life. My life.

It enabled me to move forward and it was good for me. The process of recovery had to start somewhere and it couldn't be where I was presently. It had to start with ridding myself of all of the things and people that continued to haunt me and keep me in that vicious cycle of abuse. Emotional, verbal, mental and to a large degree even the physical abuse that was happening at home. The time had come. There needed to be a finality to it.

*****

It wasn't so much as changing who I was during, after and from the domestic violence as it was cleansing my mind and soul from *ALL of the abuse* that I had endure in my life. All of it. That would require a complete internal overall and gutting process, which when I started, strangely left me in a place of, *Now what?*

And Who Am I?

How do I go from the ugliness of all that my life was and to a place where I have never been?

How do I live after never having done so?

It was scary and lonely and well, scary.

I also had to look at this continued desire to be accepted by *the siblings* who never really accepted me. I had to walk away from them, and all of the things that tied me to a place where I didn't belong. All of those things and those people were the past and for me to heal, I had to let all of them go so that I could stop hurting myself.

I had to learn to be alright that I had no family. That *the siblings* would not ever let me in the circle. And so I learned to forgive them and to love them at a distance.

Deep down inside, I was also still operating from the premise of proving to my mother that she was wrong about me, that I wasn't like my father. I tried to remain connected to her as much as possible, but it wasn't happening for a variety of reasons. All of the things that I had no control over, including *the siblings.*

That all stopped when she died. I felt relieved. No longer did I have to prove anything to anyone and my connection to the siblings were severed completely and that made me happy.

It may sound crazy to a person who has had the love of their mother, but to those of us who never had maybe not so much. Please don't write or ask me "how can I say such a thing" please don't tell me "you only get one mother". I didn't have the luxury of a mother or the love, so our experiences are not the same in the mother/daughter department.

However, it was only when I began to real work on myself and also trained formally to provide services for women in trauma and in treatment that I began to get a better sense of who my mother was when she was trying to take care of seven children by herself. I soon began to understand the man-woman dynamics as they related to her, my father and my stepmother, *in all of that,* I also began to understand *why* my childhood was what it was.

I discovered that she was like so many single mothers who lacked the companionship of a partner and the other parent to help her. She did the best that she could with what her own personal situation was and from how she had been brought up. She too had a story filled with broken dreams and I now understood completely what occurred so many years ago during that court case that forever changed her. That made me less anxious the few times I was around her and able to forgive what I had thought was a deliberate attempt to crush me because I resembled my father and what their relationship was and was not.

I know that what I am speaking is not popular or perhaps not politically correct, but it is the truth and the truth is never easy and often not wanted. More importantly,

It is my truth.

Ironically, what once destroyed me became that which has begun to heal me. My past life taught me to embrace who I am even at the cost of being alone and the beauty of life by accepting it all for *what it is* and not what I wanted it to be. *Burying the delusions of the past so that I can live in the present.*

*****

I started challenging myself to use bleach again. First a capful in the dishwater, then some to clean the toilet and finally in the laundry. It took about two full years before I was able to have the bleach bottle in view.

And the smell of coffee no longer conjured up the memories that held me captive to my childhood. I was able to see a can of coffee and to smell it without breaking into a sweat and becoming claustrophobic.

There were other things that needed to die. Foods, that Type A personality, *that going along to get along.*
That wasn't me and I would no longer people please. Period.
It was time to be me for me and *who ever didn't like THIS me never liked me anyway,* so I had nothing to lose.

Then there was the color Blue.

It wasn't until I started attending the local precinct community council meetings that I began to experiment with wearing blue. Some days I would feel as if I was choking but then the more I wore blue the less I thought about why I hated the color and what it represented to me. The cross over for me was when my mother died and I wore that blue dress to her funeral. It was a moment of finality. As I write this, I remember standing over the hospital bed holding onto her legs. She was gone. She was no longer in pain and suffering. The last twenty years of her life were spent having strokes and heart attacks, battling high blood pressure and diabetes. I stood there thinking, "It is finally over. They can't hurt me anymore."

With respect to the other things and places that had haunted me for so long, I made it my business to go back to those places and walk through those neighborhoods. It was extremely difficult, but in order to become shame free, guilt free and free from the fear that once enveloped me, I had to face the past. I rode past where I lived as a child then

I crossed the street and walked past the building. As I glanced over and stared at that stoop and the one next to it, I realized that it was over. That 1374 Boston Road had nothing over me! That I was still here and that day marked the end of those memories. Eventually, I found myself where the abuse happened with the marriage. That was tough. I tip toed back into the neighborhood one bright sunny day and stood across the street from the building. As I looked up to that sixth-floor window that he held me captive in, I felt at peace and also sorry for him. I walked away knowing that it was finished. That no matter what he said or did back then, it was never about anything that I had said or done. I turned and looked back one last time knowing that I would not be visiting that grave ever again.

*****

Once I learned what death could do and how liberating the power of forgiveness was, I started giving it away to everyone that I believed wrong me. I learned something very valuable: My soul will not be held accountable for any offense that I believed was done to me unless I did not forgive the offender. It was an easy way to laying the past to rest and moving forward.

The truth be told, there were some places that I would not ever return to. There is no reason to. There are only dead things in those places. It's is the past and I cannot change anything about it except how I view it.

It was no longer just the pain that propelled me but determination to move pass my past. I was also tired of correcting people who continually referred to me as a victim. I was tired of holding on to all the things and people that didn't want or need to be held onto. After all, at that junction, I had survived my childhood and it had been well over eighteen years since I had escaped that marriage and was never in a relationship with a physically abusive person again.

My past did not define me, nor would I allow others to label me, pigeonhole me, to stagnate my growth or break my resolve to live. There had to be closure, the type that came only with death.

*****

My greatest moment of healing came when I made the following discovery: the people that I found myself around while I was married and being abused were more than likely just as ignorant about what domestic violence was as I was. *And that piece* of wisdom took my recovery process and my inner healing to another level. Looking back, I can't be angry that they didn't help me. They couldn't help me anymore than I could have helped myself.

Some are people that I miss dearly but must leave buried in the past. Others violated my trust and betrayed me and still to this day believed that they did nothing wrong. My way of dealing with them is that I learned the art of forgiveness and I forgave them. That doesn't mean that I allow them back into my space. It means that I also consider those things dead. I was also learning to forgive myself and recovering, healing and growing dictated that I learn that so that I could recover, heal and grow and also lay things to rest.

While death is final in all things, in other things it is life and for me, beautiful, and it was in this type of death, that I began to live.

26

STAY THE COURSE

IN THE MIDST OF BRAND BUILDING and at the height of the economy when non-profits were losing funding, I found myself caught in that wave of layoffs. As I job hunt and scraped by on unemployment, I continued to brand myself and decided that I was done with the whole nine to five.

Somewhere during this time that a woman who was the Vice President of a large organization in Brooklyn whom I had met five years earlier contacted me and asked if I was interested in CASAC Training. I had no idea what she was talking about and told her that I didn't have the funds to pay for it. She said if I was interested to just show up. I did.

For the next nine months three nights a week, I made my way into lower Manhattan where I learned about drugs, substance abuse and therapeutic interventions. My skills were being fine-tuned to become a Certified Alcohol and Substance Abuse Counselor.

But not really. My sole focus was my brand. I continued to carry The Manual and I continued to follow its instructions. The end goal was to be a Domestic Violence Educator.

At school, all of my papers were related to domestic violence and during my CASAC class another student there gave me some information on a program that provides intensive training on HIV. I learned everything that I could about the impact of domestic violence and persons, particularly women with HIV. That opened the door for me to provide training to professionals that worked with that population and also to educate their participants.

I was back to work.

During one of the class sessions at that program an instructor asked a question and one of the students answered by saying 'fear'. The instructor laughed and said that there is no such thing as fear.

I felt as if he slapped me when he said that. I challenged his response and he became upset and told me that he was in charge of the class and if he said that fear stands for False Expectations Appearing Real, then his word was final and called a break. Only I did not leave the class and after the last person walked out, I shared with him my experience with fear and how there was nothing false about being abused and afraid for my life.

He looked at me, then walked over to the door and closed it and this is what he said to me:

"When I was sixteen, I loved playing softball but I couldn't focus. I was always afraid that when I got back home that my mother might be dead from my father beating her. He usually came in from work drunk and after picking an argument he would beat her. When I was little, I couldn't go outside by myself but once I got old enough to, I would leave when it was time for him to come home. I know fear. I just try not to think about how it feels."

We apologized to each other and moved on.

Once I completed the CASAC training, I immediately sat for the state test and passed it. I had already enrolled and was pursuing my Graduate Degree in Criminal Justice. While that and becoming certified in related areas seemed to be at the top of my list that just wasn't the case. I continued to fine tune my brand.

My sole objective and my time was dedicated to developing my curriculum and creating a website for my program that was to come. I had already begun to be recognized as a Domestic Violence Educator and going into different venues training staff and facilitating groups and workshops on domestic violence. I tailored each depending on the agency population and operated privately for several years before going public.

*****

There is something so amazing about education when approached openly and with no expectations. It had a way of providing answers to questions that I never would have thought to ask and answers to questions I should have been asking but didn't know needed answering. My time pursuing my Graduate Degree taught me so many things that I would not have learned absent of it.

My life started to make sense through my courses and my seemly obsession with domestic violence. Every paper and project went back to domestic violence with the exception to my counter terrorism class. While in Graduate school, I was privilege to be a student of Dr. Basil Wilson PhD. who once served as Provost and Senior Vice President of Academic Affairs, John Jay College of Criminal Justice in New York, also as Chairman Department of African American Studies, Professor of

THRIVER: My Story To Tell

Political Science, Department of African American Studies, John Jay College of Criminal Justice, among other prestigious positions. He has written extensively on violence and has produced and co-produced numerous articles and publications, including several relating to New York City. For my internship, I became one of his Research Assistants and because of that experience I was able to produce a Compassion Analysis Essay on the drop in homicides in the nineteen nineties and the level of domestic violence femicides during that same time period. It was an honor being under his tutelage and in his classes. I believe he is proud of how I turned out.

As I sat through the juvenile delinquency course, it was like almost surreal. *How it all made sense with my kids!*

Risk factor and protective factor are associated with the criminal justice field and probably some others that are intertwined. The connection with the two terms are the kids and how each can determine an outcome for children who are exposed to violence within their households.

Everything made sense.

You see, although my kids had no business in that environment, there they were. As an abused mom, I never considered how it was impacting them. After all, every Christmas there was a tree and there were presents. Exactly what they wanted. Every Easter dressed to the nines with their Easter Basket and my son, well, he still wanted his until about ten. Birthday parties, after school program, swimming lessons, karate lessons, summer camps and trips out of town. They had everything that children could want and all of their basic needs and most of their wants were met. But not really. The violence outweighed the calm and replaced what could have been wonderful childhood memories.

It wasn't until many years after they had begun to hit their late teens that I discovered that all that stuff meant nothing. That their needs were not being met because they were living in a dangerous and volatile environment. They had minimal protective factors and were at risk. I really wasn't in a position to help them. Heck, I couldn't help myself back then and was just learning how to now.

My life as a survivor of intimate partner and domestic violence *finally* began to make sense and equally important, *how I got there and why.*

My children's behavior and reactions also made sense. *Finally, I knew how to help them.*

While in school there was this one professor that hated all things domestic violence and even went as far as telling another student who worked in the field that victims are attention seeking and want pity. I had to excuse myself from the class because a drive by was about to happen. When it came time for the two of us to present our projects, he decided to not let us and said that he was confident that we did the research and that we were exempt. I didn't argue with him. All I wanted was to be done with his class.

It was people like him also who pushed me to persevere, to become stronger and do more than just survive.

*****

Work, Family, School, church. Volunteer.

That was my life for five years until my last semester of graduate school when the domestic violence residue showed up again as it often does every few years.

Short version. Everything came to a screeching halt. I ended up with custody of my first grandson who is high functioning Autistic. It was totally unexpected and changed all of my plans for post graduate school. Having him wasn't difficult since I had worked for nine years with children with special needs, including Autism. What was difficult was accepting what had happened, how he ended up with me and what was I going to do now that I had to readjust my three-year plan.

About a year and a half later with my life totally different from the responsibilities of my grandson, having re worked my plans and incorporating him into them, I pressed the reset button and return back to the world of domestic violence education and advocacy in full force while continuing to upgrade my presentation.

God was in the midst of it all.

*****

It was somewhere during this time period that I was re-introduced to the world of the New York City Police Department and oh how much things had changed within the department with respect to domestic violence. This time I was not filing a complaint and stood at that podium inside the Muster Room at the Forty Third Precinct. As I was introduced to speak for National Domestic Violence Awareness Month that particular night, I felt faint and somewhat embarrassed as I made my way up to the front. Looking back into the audience made me grip the side of the podium.

When I first started speaking publicly, I would write down what I thought matched the event. However, once I opened my mouth something completely different would come and that is exactly what happened that night.

THRIVER: My Story To Tell

I'm not too certain what I said but it must have gone over well because everyone was clapping including the officers.

It was a defining moment which could have been ruined by the actions of two individuals who cornered me outside afterwards to inform me that I was infringing on their territory as far as domestic violence is concern and actually told me not to get too comfortable. After the initial shock wore off three weeks later, I was thankful that they did exactly what they did: Strengthen me to continue and pushed me to *stay the course*.

From there, I am not quite sure when it happened or how, but I had gone from attending monthly community council meetings at the local precinct to being nominated for position of Recording Secretary on the Executive Board. I ran uncontested and won on the night my second grandson was being born.

I got to know the officers and Domestic Violence Officers there and although I am no longer there, I hold them all in high esteem. They understand the whys. They know the smells. They see the broken furniture and torn clothes and the holes in the walls and the blood and the broken bodies and destroyed children.

As First Responders, they more so than anyone outside of that unit, understand the dynamics of domestic violence.

A year after that I was asked to attend 'an application party' in Brooklyn and initially I balked. I didn't want to travel that far but it was one of the best professional moves made. My extensive knowledge of domestic violence put me at an advantage and that made me an asset to the NYSOARS ATR 3 Grant. When I was approved as a Provider with the NYSOARS ATR III Grant under OASAS, it was then that I realized that something big was happening and when I received my Visit Coach

Certification, that really put into perspective how far I had come from being that abused and neglected child.

None of it seemed real and as I completed one training or the next, I would tuck the paper work or diploma away in a bin and move to the next course.

Truth be told, as easily as the doors swung open for each opportunity, there was the hard work to be put in to fully take advantage of each opportunity presented.

Hard because I was still struggling with the aftershocks from the abuse.

I spent many days operating on three to four hours of rest and operating at that level left no time to think about the past.

That and taking care of my grandson.

27

READY

WHEN I STARTED SPEAKING AT PUBLIC events on domestic violence many years ago, I did not believe that I was prepared for all of this but someone else did.

Invited to speak at event in Brooklyn at a church many years ago, feeling dejected, naked and beaten afterwards, I made my way back to the Bronx. Several months later, I received a call from a woman who had gotten my number from someone at the previous Brooklyn event. She said that her church was looking for someone to give their testimony about how God had rescued them and redeemed them.

That is what she said but not what I heard. I heard that they wanted me to tell my story for their benefit. I told her that I needed few days to think about it and she said don't think about it too long.

I ended up speaking at this event, giving my testimony that is. There were three of us that night and after service was done and the refreshments were being eaten, an elderly woman walked up to me and pointed her finger right at me and said, *"You. You are ready."*

"Excuse me? I replied, *"Ready for what?"*

"You are ready.", she said again.

"Ready to do the work. I listened to you speak several months ago. I am the person that contacted you to be here this evening. I am here to tell you tonight that you are healed and you are ready. You don't know the strength your words have.

That is good. You are ready."

We engaged in a private conversation for about 20 minutes or so and then I left and headed back home and away from her. I never did see her again, but her words began to haunt me. *Ready for what?*

*****

Fast forward five years. The voice message simply said that if I was interested in sharing my story as a survivor to give them a call back. Still creating a place for myself publicly in this field, I accepted the invite and six weeks later was sitting in the third row with my daughter waiting for my turn to speak.

The two women behind us started talking about how they hate being sent to these domestic violence events. Then one of them said something that changed how I forever would tell my story.

One asked the other how was her case going and the other started complaining how she couldn't stand to go to that house. She continued on about how dirty the house looked and smelled and that the children got on her nerves. Her co-worker asked what was she going to do about it and she said she was going to be asked to be switched to another case especially since she was tired of the mother not doing what she needed to do to leave the man that was beating her.

I couldn't believe that I was hearing this conversation. In a public venue.

They were supposed to be professionals, service providers for those that needed, well, services.

They had no clue that I was one of the guest presenters because I did not sit with the other speakers.

Or that I was once one of the clients that was pathetic and just needed to leave that man who was beating me.

*****

After being introduced, the first thing I did was asked the audience,

>"What does domestic violence look like?"
>"Who can be a victim of domestic violence?"
>Then I said, *"Let's play a game.*
>
>*I need four volunteers. Each one of you are students in the fourth grade and today is What Do You Want To Be Day. I will first be the Teacher, then the fifth student."*

As we went through the exercise with each saying a typical response, doctor, cop, nurse, teacher, suddenly, I yelled out really loudly,

>"Me! Me! I know what I want to be!
>
>"I want to be a Victim of Domestic Violence!
>
>*I want my boyfriend to beat me and I want him to call me all types of nasty names and make me feel worthless*

and unloved AND I want everybody to judge me and blame me because I want to be a victim of domestic violence!!"

Where people were first laughing they suddenly stopped and everyone sat there shocked.

Shocked because listening to a person say that they want to be a victim of domestic violence just solidified how ludicrous it is to believe that people who are being abused, aspired to be in that position.

It was time to begin my presentation.

I then disclosed that many years prior to me standing in front of them that I was indeed a victim of intimate partner violence and that I had not aspired to become one. That no one, not one single person that I have ever met had deliberately set their minds and made it their goal to be abused, beaten or sexually assaulted by their partner.

The next forty-five minutes left to my presentation focused on how parenting skills are negatively impacted by domestic violence and how the children in those violent households often learn to fend for themselves because the abused parent can't and people who are outside looking in won't.

I told my sons' story and I told my youngest daughters' story then I turned and faced the two women in the fourth row that were sitting behind where I sat.

I looked directly at them and told the audience how no mom wants her children in that situation and that the children don't want their mom in that situation and how these children grow up with torn loyalties for both parents and how some of these children grow up to hate the parent that is being abused.

And often grow up to hate themselves for many reasons, including for not being able to help the abused parent.

And when I had finished, I thank everyone for bearing with me, that I had not come there that day to speak like that and if I offended anyone, I apologize. The organizer who was also the Director of the agency looked at me and walked out of the room.

People applauded and the two women got up and left and as I went to sit back down a break was called. The organizer came back into the room and pulled me to the side. She turned her back to the group, looked over her shoulder then back at me and said,

"You were talking about me. As you were telling your sons' story, I saw myself running for help and no one helped.

No one ever talks about the kids. I was one of those kids and I had to step out of the room to compose myself. Thank you for sharing my story.

All of these years later I still can't talk about watching my father beat my mother. Thank you for talking about how domestic violence is for the kids.

No one ever talks about the kids."

I stood there not knowing what to say, how do I set this right. It wasn't my intention to open up any wounds. She must have read my mind because she then said,

"It is okay. I feel better than I have in many years. To know that I wasn't alone and to hear someone stick up for the kids. Thank you."

We hugged and took a picture. Then others began sharing bits and pieces of their stories and of how inspired they were and there were some officers there as well. Two others came up to me and after thanking me, both said that they had become Domestic Violence Officers because their moms were victims of domestic violence when they were children. As the break was ending a man walked over to me, shook his head and said, *"I didn't get it until today. I didn't understand until I saw your son running down that hallway. Your story was so vivid. I get it."* He walked off without another word.

That night when I reflected back on my day, I knew that telling my story required me to tell it truthfully, without shame and from the victims' perspective.

It was that day that I discovered that the only way that people who have never experience being abused or victimized will ever even begin to grasp the significance of what victims endure is to tell it from a victim's perspective.

Real and raw and with no apologies.

Back to that pivotal moment in Brooklyn five years ago, that woman's voice came back to me, *You're ready.*

Now I understood.

28

IN MY LIVING ROOM

SUNSHINE IN MY LIVING ROOM WAS borne out of my personal experience with intimate partner violence and domestic violence.

As the CEO and Founder of Sunshine In My Living Room, I have had and continue to have the immense privilege of educating, advocating and bringing awareness about what domestic violence is and *is not*, and also how men factor into intimate partner violence from both sides, as the abuser and as the abused.

My *Speak Up* Campaign is two-fold. One, to Advocate through education and awareness for those whose voice has been stripped from them due to intimate partner violence and sexual violence without watering it down or trying to beautify what it is and two, to inspire others to inspire others, through my journey.

*****

I lived up on the top floor of the building at Five Seventy Five East One Hundred Fortieth Street in the Bronx. That was back in the days when that neighborhood was rough and tough. A lot of crazy things happen in that community even in broad daylight. And also in that sun filled living room of my apartment way up there on the sixth floor.

The living room windows of the apartment sat directly on the corner of the building unobstructed. When the sun rose in the morning, no matter where it travelled, on any given day, no matter where it was perched in the sky, its bright shine and beaming rays found its way into that living room. Everyone who visited loved the view from the window and how bright it was.

It was so beautiful.

But then it wasn't.

The mauve colored painted walls and the living room furniture were a perfect match. The three- piece couch set was black with mauve and light grey flowers strategically placed. Baby pictures adorned the wall and at Christmas time, monogramed stockings overlooked the tree that was encircled with presents. On one side of the room stood an entertainment center and on the other end of this large room was a beautiful black lacquer dining table with four matching chairs with mauve colored cushions sprinkled with tiny black dots. There were lots of plants and pictures in both of the windows and the white tiled floor was partially covered with an enormous oriental rug that held the same colors as the furnishings and the wall. The kids loved to sit on while watching television. It was a living room filled to the brim with sunshine.

A beautiful room that was also filled with such horrible, horrible memories.

THRIVER: My Story To Tell

That particular day as I stood in the debris from the dining table that laid crumbled on the floor, broken in half from his drunken rage the night before, I thought about, that even with all of the sunlight that is always in this room, it was *always so dark*. The mangled chairs down at my feet authenticated the level of destruction that had taken place and was now waiting for me to do something with the mess.

The things that took place *in that room, in that window* obscured the brightness of the sun. It blocked out any light and any joy that otherwise could have made that such a wonderful living environment. I thought about the sunshine in that living room and how if I ever told anyone what really happened there, no one will probably believe me.

The many days spent mopping blood off of the white tiled floor all the while unable to feel the warmth of the sun that streamed through the windows. The mauve colored semi-gloss paint allowed for the blood splatters to wipe off easily without leaving stains and the smell of Clorox always permeated the entire apartment. The scent from the constant use of bleach part of the norm.

The sun would just sit there until it set in the evening and some days I would pull down the shades and then hang bed sheets over them to prevent the sun from entering the space. It was too bright and almost felt like it had no business there. Often, I would turn the music up as loudly as possible to drown out the emotions that crept over me every time I entered or passed through that room. The years went by and the abuse continued but I never forgot about that sunshine in my living room and in spite of the darkness that had settled in it, there was a quiet beauty to it. I could almost feel it.

THRIVER: My Story To Tell

Almost. But not quite.

As someone who have survived multiple trauma and ultimately found my voice through my journey of healing, I believe that it is crucial that the voice of those who lives have been severely impacted by domestic violence is heard.

All too often when information is disseminated it is done from a professional standpoint. The information is clinical and unrealistic to those who are being abused and for many who have survived abuse. The real experts are the ones who survived. *Their voices matter. Our voices matter.* They understand what Safety Planning is about based on *their* circumstances. They, like myself, knows what works and what doesn't work.

This does not take away from those who have dedicated their professional lives to effect change and make a difference. What it should do is bring the affected party to the table instead of leaving them to sit in the hall while being discussed. Recognizing, respecting and incorporating the experience and voice of victims and survivors could bridge the chasm that continues to discount what those who are being abused have to offer to both their healing recovery and for those that are still being abused. I believe it is one way to work toward reducing the number of incidences. That and enforcing the laws while also offering and providing therapeutic options to offenders which include other options besides the model currently in play. It doesn't work.

We, the abused, the formerly abused, the families of the abused, the professionals, law enforcement and society as large, we all know what the abuse look like and sounds like. We know the difficulty that the abused go through in terms of how their life is controlled and that each choice they make can be their last.

Advocating, educating, training, and telling my story, in any form, is not about the darkness but the light, the hope that there is life after domestic violence. It is not just about *where* I have been but also my journey to where I am.

This work is not for the faint hearted or the frightened.

It is for those of us who understand that there will be times that we must stand alone because others are too concerned with stepping on toes or their image.

It is for of us who recognize that we can't help everyone and that not everyone will like or trust us.

It is about those who are currently in that precarious situation of being a victim and a survivor at the same time while also being voiceless.

It is about them, their children *and their families*.

This work is also not about me.

That is the thought that stays at the forefront of my mind.

It is about those who are in need of information, inspiration, empowerment and resources for whatever degree of violence that they or their love one may be experiencing.

For me, it is *always, always a privilege* for me that a person would allow me into their deepest and darkest secrets birthed from tragedy and trauma. My credentials and professional training does not entitle me to be a part of their journey and it is only my personal experience that resonate with them which allows me to.

For me to be a part of their journey, is always an honor, a privilege and *never, ever a given.*

Sunshine In My Livingroom at its' essence is about *Speaking Up Against Domestic Violence.*

It is about dispelling the myths and sharing the facts.

It is about shattering the darkness that steals the voices of the abused, that robs them of their hope for tomorrow, that crushes their spirit from the shame and the blame.

It is about advocating and teaching self-advocacy.

It is about standing up and not backing down and challenging the status quo on how domestic violence is talked about.

It is about being real, raw and radical enough to shock the sensibilities with the truth about what domestic violence / intimate partner violence is *and is not.*

Speaking Up brings to light the hidden things and strips secrets of their power.

29

I AM GWEN....NOT

AS I CROSSED THE STREET A woman looked me up and down and said, *"Gwen?, Oh my God! Everyone thought you were dead! You just vanished and the rumors were that he killed you!"*

I smiled and said, *"Hi. How are the kids? I know that they're all grown since our kids are the same age and by the way, I don't go by Gwen anymore. My name is Doreen."*

"Doreen? Oh. Okay. But what happened to you. Where did you go?'

"It was time for a change and time for me to go. Like now. It was great seeing you." I walked off without answering her questions. She was one of the neighbors who lived in the building and knew all too well what my life was like back when. I felt bad afterwards. I must remember that she probably didn't know any better.

*****

Gwendolyn is my middle name and everyone who met me at any point of my former marriage, knew me as Gwen. That is another story for another book. Gwen as everyone called me was definitely a different person than I am. She was all too trusting and wore rose colored glasses, even to bed. She was naïve and vulnerable. But her uncanny ability to weather all the storms that came her way and remain standing still shocks me. I mean when I glance back to those ten years it amazes me that she did not have a mental breakdown. The sheer level of responsibilities that were part of her life as a mother was enormous and then to add the abuse. Wow.

I don't think of me, Doreen, when I think of Gwen. We really are two different people. Yes, I know it sounds weird.

It's just that it is hard to identify with who I was back then.

*****

The phone rang and it was his niece informing me that my ex father in law had passed away. It had been nearly six years since I had spoken to any of them. She provided us with the details and we went to the service. Sitting there I couldn't help but wonder, exactly what did his father really do for a living that the mere mention of his name would send the officers away?

As my children and I exited the funeral parlor, the family was entering the family car to go to the cemetery, my ex spouse told me to get inside, that I was family. I shook my head and kept walking. There absolutely no way that was going to happen. About two nights later, my phone rang again and this time it was him.

"Hi Gwen", He said, as if all was well. Like nothing had *ever* happened.

"My name is not Gwen, my name is Doreen. What do you want."

Sure, I could have hung up that phone as soon as I recognized his voice. I could have. But I didn't.

"Damn Baby, why are you being so mean. I just want to talk to you. I've been thinking about you, about us and I wanted to know if we can go away together."

In my head, I snapped. This person had beat me off and on for eight years, then spent an entire year refusing to sign off on the divorce papers. This person who terrorized me and terrorized my children. This person who had strangled me unconscious and almost murdered me on three separate occasions. This person who stalked me for eighteen months after I left him, and while he didn't find me, it was horrifiying with him terrorizing me and contacting my employee trying to get me fired.

And you want me to go away with you? All of that went through my head in about fifteen seconds.

"Let me explain something to you. You know that little girl that you used to be married to?" I asked. And before he could utter a word, I said, *"She's dead and I killed her. "She doesn't exist anymore and my advice to you is to not contact Me ever again. If you do, you will be sorry because I know where you live and you will have a problem."*

"Wow, it's not that serious. I just wanted to spend some time with you", he said.

"Let me make myself perfectly clear: I am not Gwen and you will never have the opportunity of spending time with me. If you contact me again, you will have

problems," I said in no uncertain terms and I hung up my phone.

I had arrived. I was stronger and just as that woman had said so many years ago in Brooklyn.

I was ready.

Maybe three or four years later he tried contacting me again. I gave him no air time whatsoever. I informed him that he is not to contact me or I would file a complaint with NYPD and when he called me again, that is exactly what I did. I never heard from him again.

But I did hear about him.

*****

Two days before my birthday in twenty fifteen as I laid sick in bed with the flu, I kept receiving texts from my Big Girl.

Get the paper. Get the paper. Get the paper.
The texts kept coming in.

This must have gone on for about 30 minutes. I was not getting out of my bed and going outside in that cold to get a paper, until she finally sent a text that said:

Your ex-husband is in the paper. The Post.

A split second later a friend from Georgia texted the same thing: *Your ex-husband is in the newspaper.*

I flew out the bed put on a long coat and boots and ran out the apartment. I ran from store to store until I found the paper. Looking like a mad woman in the cold February air with no winter clothes on, I started tearing through the paper looking for the article.

There it was. *There was the article.*

It happened at his parents' home. and there was his mother quoted as saying he didn't do it.

I didn't have to see him do it. I lived with him *and the terror.* I know what he is capable of.

The news said he squirted lighter fluid in a woman's face then set her face on fire.

I screamed and ran out of the store and back home.
The article said that they couldn't find him. I called the precinct in that area and asked to speak to the detective assigned.

And yes, I identified myself as his ex wife.

When the detective came to the phone, I asked if they were still looking for him and she said no.

That he had been caught. In that moment, I was overjoyed!! I began jumping up and down and shouting *"Yes! "Hallelujah! Hallelujah",* until I realized that I was still holding the phone with the detective on the other end.

"My apologies", I stammered then hung up.

That was short lived because of *why* he was arrested. No one deserves to be set on fire. Not for any reason.

I wept for her.

It is my prayer that one day she will heal internally and emotionally from that horrendous act of violence.

Then I went into a panic. Oh No!! Baby Gurl!

I had to refocused and get my mind straight and find the right words to tell my Baby Gurl that he had been arrested and why before she hears it from somewhere else.

But it was too late. One of her professors connected the last name and the resemblance and even asked her if she knew the man in the article. She didn't go back to class for two weeks.

We were dragged back into our past and it took a minute to regroup. Maybe ten minutes. Okay it took about a month. *We just couldn't seem to get away from him.*

And just when I thought it was over again, *I was wrong.* I was heading home and as the train was pulling into my stop, my cell rang from an unknown number.

"Hello?"
"Hello. Can I speak with Doreen Lesane, please."
"This is she, who am I speaking with?'

"Hi. I'm calling from the Bronx District Attorney Office," he voice on the other line said.

THRIVER: My Story To Tell

It was about *him. Why can't I get away from this person? Really?*

We had a conversation about the status of his current criminal case and I was asked if I would be willing to testified against him at the next court date. I stated my position on that and that what his violent tendencies were well documented and that public information that could be located in the court record room. As we were winding down our conversation, she then asked,

"Who is Gwen? The name keeps coming up and he seems to think that the only reason that the court is offering him thirty years is because of this woman named Gwen. I thought that you were his only ex-wife."

I took a deep breath. *"I am Gwen."*

"I mean that is my middle name and it is what everyone used to call me."

Including my other abuser.

His sister.

*****

She was mean and nasty and *never* had a kind word to say to me. I couldn't quite figure out why and I never asked her. She always made derogatory remarks about my skin tone or my weight. You know, how light skinned women aged faster than dark skinned women or how yellow girls think they better.

Please don't let me and food be in the same space, the comments then became about how skinny I was or 'how skinny chicks think ya'll all that'. It was a constant barrage of insults and her family said nothing. He said nothing. Normally, I said nothing.

It is my belief that she would deliberately set things in motion for her brother to attack and abuse me.

Perfect example, I don't wear make -up. I don't, now or ever feel that little girls under thirteen should wear nail polish. That is me and my choice. That choice pertained to my daughters when they were little girls.

When my two older daughters were six and three, my former in laws took them home with them after church one Sunday. When I went to pick them up, their nails were polished and I expressed my displeasure. The sister who painted them and I had already had a conversation about me not wanting any make up, including nail polish on them. Several conversations actually.

She stated that they were her nieces (actually only by marriage) and that she could paint their nails if she wanted to. Well, I disagreed and took my girls and went home. Later that evening, he comes over, like all is well and well, I thought all was well. The girls came out of their room and said hi and he kind of played with them, asked them how was their visit at the grandparents and then asked to see their nails.

"Mommy said we had to take it off", my six-year old daughter said.

"That's okay. Take your sister back in the room. I want to talk with your Mom."

He walked them to their room and closed the door behind them then walked over to where I was sitting and

the next thing I know is that he had yanked me out of my seat by my hair and began slamming my head into the wall. As this was going on all that I could think of is *"what did I do'.*
    Literally.

    In that moment as he was banging my head into the wall, the only thoughts *were what did I do.* Even as I sit and write about it, the memories of the pain doesn't register. It happened so swiftly
    It was almost as if he read my mind. He began yelling, *"How dare you disrespect my sister! Who the hell do you think you are!".*

    When the babies came running out of the room crying he started telling them that I started with him.

    That he was trying to talk to me about why did I clean the pretty polish off of their hands and that I attacked him.
    Years later as I sit and try to help other victims/survivors make sense of their journey, I hear that one theme over and over again. His mother knew. His father knew. His sister, his brother, his niece, his nephew. *Everyone knew.*
    And the person who talks about how the abuser family member knew often talks about how that family member did one of three things: Nothing, condone it, or became that persons' Secondary Batterer and abused the person as well.
    From that moment on I had my daughters around her a little as possible, however, she never changed her attitude towards me and long after I divorced her brother when our paths crossed, she still felt the need to be her. She

continued to call me Gwen although I told her that wasn't my name or who I am.

I have, on many occasions, crossed paths with his sister but no longer stop to speak with her and don't acknowledge her.

I used to maybe once or twice and each time her choice of conversation is about her brother.

That ship has sail and I was on it.

The end had come for any relationship with that family.

Those are dead things.

It is not because I hate them or harbor any ill will.

It is because just like I have forgiven my former spouse, I have also forgiven them and moved on.

As Doreen.

30

A MATTER OF OPINION

I WAS INVITED TO THE RADIO show to speak about Domestic Violence and thank God that I was able to hold my own. As I sat there with the mic in my hand, I watched the two other guests on the other side of the desk. The two men challenged every statement that I made, and one had the audacity to try to tell me *how I should feel* as a black woman.

Just as we returned to the air from a break, the loud one goes straight for the jugular. I think that he was trying to intimidate me but that wasn't going to happen. Not this day.

"Well, as a black woman, you should be outraged at how society allows this crime to happen to other black women.", he bellowed at me.

I continued to lean back in my seat, smiled at him and then calmly stated, *"It is not about being a black woman. Domestic violence doesn't discriminate and happens to people of all nationalities and genders. As an educator, it is about domestic violence and its impact on communities....."*

"Wait a minute Ms. Lesane, are you disavowing your race?!! Are you trying to say that domestic violence doesn't impact communities of color disproportionately?"

"What I am saying is that you are calling me a black woman.

I am a woman and my ethnicity should have no bearing if I was a victim of a crime.

As a matter of fact, it is my belief that the perpetuation of separating, categorizing, and labeling victims is exactly how this specific atrocity continues to happen at the rate that it does.

When society starts to focus on what is happening based on ethnicity, gender, sexuality when does it have the time to find real solutions that will work for the victims?'

He sat there with a smirk on his face as I continued…

"You say that I am a black woman."

"I say that I am a woman. Your attempt to define me by a label and your belief system with regards to domestic violence may be your choice, however, I say this to you…you are entitled to your opinion and your beliefs system but only what I say who I am defines me.

I have survived domestic violence and now advocate against it not as a black woman but as a person.

The saying 'Domestic Violence doesn't discriminate' is proven truth. Anyone, anywhere can be a victim. It does not care where you live or how you look. It doesn't care how much money you have or don't have. It doesn't look at your skin tone or ethnicity.

Any. Human. being. At any age. From anywhere.

So, for me, this is not a skin tone issue.
It is a human issue and it is a crime.
And crimes, like domestic violence, does not discriminate either.

He looked at me, smiled, shook his head and then it was his partner turn.

At the end of the show, we all shook hands and laughed.
"No hard feelings, right? I needed to see if you knew your stuff and if you could hold your own. Good job", he said. *When I grow up I want to be just like you."*

"Thank you and None at all. I expected nothing less when I walked through the doors of this studio.", I said.

*****

This Domestic violence issue is so beyond nationality, gender, ethnicity or sexuality. It goes beyond which population or community is more impacted or who hurts the worse. It is not about living urban, suburban or country. It transcends all of that.

I know that there are those who will respectively disagree and there will be those that vehemently disagree. I am fine with both views.

Through personal and professional experience and exposure, I have learned that the more divided, the more trying to one up the next culture or community about how bad domestic violence is to one person or the other is the reason why it will never be combatted. It will never be eradicated because it is approached all wrong.

From sitting in the audience listening to others share their story of abuse to engaging with those seeking assistance and resources to participating and recalling my own experience, all of the stories have the same theme. All have the same angst, the same story of pain, fear, isolation, betrayal, shame, disappointment, confusion, feelings of worthlessness and self-blame. All face judgment from family and society and *a lack of support.* All face barriers to leaving the abuse including lack of services due to lack of funding. All have or had the same fears, the same reservations. All face or faced the same challenges, just at different levels and different degrees.

All have one thing in common: *None signed up* to be abused or victimized by their partners or by society.

What separates them is their own personal experience, their reality of their situation. The details of what is happening or has happened to them. Their personal experience of being abused. They are all victims of a crime and while it is difficult for some to grasp the concept of being a survivor as they are being abused, they are. If you lived through that moment of the physical abuse, you survived that moment.

The separation into different categories and nationalities only serve the abuser.

As long as society continues to categorize which "communities of domestic violence victims face the most challenges", none of those communities will receive adequate assistance.

Fighting this evil is not about ethnicity, gender or sexuality.

It is about people.

The only thing that separates me from others that has survive being brutally abused is my own personal experience and my own personal response, my reality to what was my situation for all of those years and how I now choose to respond to that chapter of my life.

I, too, have sought help at an agency that catered to another ethnicity other than mine and was turned away. My ethnicity determined whether or not I was eligible to receive services, which I did not. This is real and it sends victims back into abusive situations.

I have heard it said and read the statistics that a woman leaves approximately seven times before finally leaving an abusive relationship and while there are reasons why she returns, the lack of adequate services or the re victimization from the systems designed to assist, is never mentioned.

I was one of those statistics.

Those reasons are real and valid and many times comes from that abused woman not meeting the criteria for assistance, thus forcing her and her children to return back to the abuse.

While this is my story to tell, it is also the story of others like me. *It is our story.* The story of the countless, voiceless, hopeless and faceless victims who are isolated, revictimized, stigmatized and shamed into staying and many times forced back to where the abusers are and some, ultimately killed.

Not just by their abuser but also by the shame and blame that society levies upon them.

It happened to me. To my 'clients' and to those who I come across almost on a daily basis. The stories are all the same.

During my quest to get away, my family became a statistic and I don't believe that it was because of low self-esteem (victim blaming).

I find in my current work that as I listen to women, men, teens and young adults who have survived domestic violence, their journey is strikingly similar. The mistrust of people, what society considers paranoia, the self- isolation and self-blame, the inability to manage their finances, the dress up garbage can syndrome and yes, even the church hurt.

Many people, both professionals and regular people like to use this as a way of explaining why women end up in unhealthy and abusive relationships: low self-esteem.

The low esteem that they suffer from is something that is bestowed upon them through abuse and blame.

This is my opinion about self-esteem as it relates to victims/survivors of domestic violence that I posted in response to a post on social media about why victims of domestic violence don't leave and immediately someone said, *"Exactly and self-esteem"*, I responded by writing this:

(This is exactly how I posted it.)

"Esteem is defined as RESPECT, ADMIRATION toward others.

So self-esteem is about respecting one self.

A woman (person) who is Being Abused by ANOTHER PERSON is BEING DISRECTED by *THAT* person…..*the abuser., the accuser*

It is difficult for a VICTIM to feel good about themselves when they are (have been) being tortured, beaten, sexually violated, financially abused, judged, blamed, laughed at, shunned, isolated, abandoned by family and "friends", degraded in front of their children and neighbors.

How VALUED does this woman (person) feel…how can she even BEGIN to ADMIRE anything about herself when she is (has been) hopeless and in THE STRUGGLE OF HER LIFE?

Staying because of low self-esteem?

Victim Blaming.

This common myth that women STAY because they have low or no self-esteem is just another way of Blaming the Victim.

This is just ANOTHER REASON WOMEN CONTINUE TO BE BEATEN, RAPED AND VICTIMIZED not just by their abusers *but ALSO* by society.

No one Wants, Chooses or Deserves to be Abused.

Not anyone that I have talked to or work with in the 10 years that I have being doing this work.

Not anyone that I have met on this journey call Life.

Not even me."

The person never spoke to me again. I' m sorry she felt that way, but I must speak the truth as I see it and as I lived it.

People just don't get it: It is NOT the victims' fault that they are being abused. I also hear this often from those that I come in contact with as well, how they feel treated "less than" once they mention that they are or have been abused.

Each time I apologize to them.

And I remind them that what happened or is happening to them was not or is not their fault. That the abuse never was their fault and never will be. That people outside of the experience don't always get it, but please don't let that stop your healing process.

I remind them that the person who is responsible is the person that abused them.

It is often a difficult concept to process and many struggle with believing the abuse is not their fault.

It took me a while to process that statement as well.

31

A DRIVE BY

EVERY NOW AND THEN MY STUFF from the past gets kicked up and my emotions do a drive by. My mouth becomes my weapon of choice.

I am not going to pretend that I am perfectly free from my past and that life is sweet and all that other good stuff. I am still in recovery from all of the abuse that I have suffered. From childhood straight thru my thirties, is more than a lifetime and thank God, that He was there for me. Living on guard was not easy and exhausting mentally.

And Trust? No.

Yes, healing happens, life improves, however, life is *never* just life again. Trauma has a way of cementing that fact.

I had to and *continue to work* on the things that triggers me the most and set off my alarm to where I find myself doing a drive by with my mouth.

I continue to work on feeling safe so that I can continue to thrive.

I continue to work on staying away from people that do not have my best interest at heart.

They are not hard to spot.

People are people with their own issues and their own human frailties. Hurt people hurt people unconsciously as I like to say.

I get that but that *doesn't justify allowing someone to hurt or take advantage of me.*

I was once one of those hurt persons and had no problem being reckless with my mouth. Yes, haunted by my past and blinded by my pain and believe me, it wasn't pretty.
It was my way of protecting me. I wasn't going to let *anyone,* no one treat me bad again for any reason.

At that time, that was the best that I could do giving my circumstances. Now that I know better I strive to do better. I am no longer that person *or* the one who will allow someone to hurt me.

To anyone and everyone that I offended with hurtful words, I am truly sorry. I did not mean to and I apologize.

Please know that I continue to work on myself and those drive bys.

*****

That day, going through my social media page, I saw several postings with people posing and smiling captioned with "*Look at me. I got my purple on for DV awareness*".
I don't know what happened. I felt heat rising from my feet up to my head. I couldn't contain my emotions and thought about declining the invite to speak at the local community board that evening.

No. I would go. I had to go.

I got dressed and left for the meeting and arrived early enough to take a time out and cool down.

When I entered the room, there were about a hundred or so people already seated. I sat as close to the door as I possibly could, trying to soothe my emotions and not let them get the best of me.

He walked in and cams directly up to me and said, *"Hey Doreen, I see that you're representing.'*

Yes, I had my purple on but for a different reason than everyone else.

"Not really", I stated tersely.

"You speaking tonight?", he asked.

"I am supposed to"

"Hmm. Are you okay? you seem a little out of sorts"

"I fine", I replied and turned away.

As he walked away, I contemplated leaving the venue and as I did, the meeting came to order.

When it was my turn to speak, I marched up to the front of the room and positioned myself where I would be dead center to everyone there.

I began talking about the purple ribbon that was pinned on my purple sweater. I told the audience that I would not be giving them out as I had done in the past years. That at an event several weeks ago, the ribbons were given out and later on into the event the floor of the venue was scattered with the little purple ribbons and that I had watched several people who had asked for one, take them off after taking pictures and dropped them on the floor.

My conversation then turned to how most people perceive the color purple to represent domestic violence awareness. Actually, I declared, the color purple represents and is associated with royalty and being regal and there is *nothing* royal or regal about domestic violence unless you count the purple necklace that a victim wears around her throat after being strangled within an inch of her life or that purple ring around the eye from being punched in it.

I unbutton the purple cardigan that I had on and flung that on the floor stating that I would no longer wear purple during the month of October. Awareness surrounding domestic violence should be every month since it happens every day. Or every fifteen seconds as the stats say. I proceeded to state that statistics by saying seventy five percent of the United States population knows someone who is being or has been abused. Included in those numbers are the children who are standing on the corner, truant from school, runaways, those forced out by the violence, the ones that society label as menaces, and thugs and out of control. ...... *"Bzzzz."*

The timer went off. I had exceeded my three minutes.

I turned around and a looked at the district manager.

"Go ahead Doreen. The floor is yours."

I picked up right where I left off.

"Many of these teenagers and young adults live in the same building that this audience lives in and many sitting in this audience knows for a fact that one or the other parent is being abused.

Yet that child is judged and like the abused parent responsible for the violence that is being perpetrated against that family.

And no one says anything.

THRIVER: My Story To Tell

The silence continues as people organizes, attends and pretends that National Domestic Violence Awareness Month is a holiday to celebrate and to honor victims."

I stopped and looked around the room and ended by saying,

"What qualifies me to stand here and say all of this is that I was a victim. I survived domestic violence. My children survived domestic violence and were like the children who are now being judged. My children lives were not just destroyed by my former batterer but by every neighbor who refused to let their children play with mine because I was being beaten and for no other reason.

And as silent as each of you are now is the same silence that allows this crime to continue. Thank you."

I picked up the purple ribbon and my purple sweater and walked straight towards the exit, opened the garbage can and tossed the ribbon inside.

No one said a word, just watched as I made my way back to my seat. I opened the backpack that I had carried with me and pulled out a pair of black boots and an army fatigue jacket and after changing from the purple boots and putting the jacket on, in my own was I was declaring war….on the color purple.

Several months after that I was approached by someone who saw me that night and she said, *"Every time I see anything purple, I think of you and what you said. It kind of changed how I thought about domestic violence."*

I smiled softly at her and said," *Thank you. That is what I hope to have happened. If only one persons' viewpoint was changed then mission accomplished."*

Needless to say, I was never invited back there and I am alright with that.

No one who was there can unhear what was said.

Yes, I will admit. It was a drive by moment. I let my emotions get the best of me and tripped up and slipped up. Still was in the process of learning how to control my emotions.

You see, while I admired Wanda Petronski from *The Hundred Dresses*. I grew up to be another girl in the book, Maddie, who decided that she would not ever stand on the sidelines and watch as others are treated badly.

She decided to *Speak Up* and so have I.

32

FLIP SIDE

AS I TRAVEL THROUGH THE CITY, I often hear how people that are being abused need to love themselves, respect themselves.

But what happens when a child comes from a place where there is no mommy or daddy? You know that place where there is no nurturing going on, where there are drugs, violence, child abuse and neglect. You know that place where the child, learns to fend for themselves and may also have to try and fend off an adult or sibling who is trying to molest them or worse is molesting them. You know that place where social skills and life skills are not taught and consider this, what happens if the child grows up and becomes a victim of intimate partner violence.

I also hear that people need to love themselves, that they need to respect themselves so that they don't continue to be a victim.

How does a person learn to love them self if they were never given love, shown love or taught what love is?

How does this person who has now become trapped in this ugly vicious cycle of abuse exercise self-respect when they were never taught, shown or given respect?

Why is it so easy for society to say that if they love themselves or have respect for themselves then they wouldn't be in that position?

Why isn't the offender, batterer, abuser being asked why don't they have any respect for themselves, their partner or the children that may be present?

Why are they not ask about their own self- hatred or lack of self-love, self-respect or insecurity?

Why is the victim being held to a higher standard than the offender?

Why can't an abuser voluntarily seek help, why can that person attend a batterers' program only if mandated?

Why are there punitive actions but no therapeutic assistance for abusers?

A sex offender can receive "help" to understand his/her actions but an abuser can't?

Why does an offender have more rights than a victim?

Just asking.

*****

"I don't care what anyone thinks! As soon as he gets out of jail, I'm going back to him. He's a good person and if I stop doing things to piss him off then he wouldn't abuse me." I stood there and said nothing.

"Guess what, my father beat my mother and he was a good person too and a good father and I still love him so I am not interested in hearing or learning about domestic violence because that don't apply to me. I just need to get myself together so that when he gets home we will be okay."

I smiled at her and said that I understood and that if she ever wanted to talk to please call me. I know that her reality was based on her life experience. No one self identifies as a victim of abuse *until they can*. This is that emotional attachment that I spoke of. She is still invested emotionally in that man regardless of the abuse. Her time had not come and that is okay. I'll be here if it does.

*****

A young man walked over to the area where I was stationed with my table at the health fair. With him were two children, a small boy and a small girl. I gave each one a lollipop.

"*Hi. How are you Today?*", I asked

"*I'm good. What type of information is this?*", he asked.

"*Domestic Violence, Teen Dating Violence.*"

"*Oh. That's not for me. I don't need this*", he said and turned to walked away.

"*Are those your kids?* I asked. He smiled at them and nodded.

"*Give me two minutes. Let me explain to you why you may need it, even if not for yourself.*"

I pointed out his two children were going to do exactly what he did, grow up and start to like someone. Maybe even start dating before he thinks that they are ready. I also mentioned that while he may have never experienced it or knew anyone who did, having the information wouldn't hurt. He stared at me for a few seconds then nodded his head. I asked him what would he say to his children when they came home and told him that they were dating. I asked, *How would you prepare them to be safe?*

"*I didn't think of it like that*", he said and put his arms around the little girl that was with him. He then took some of the literature that was laid out and said thank you. Mission accomplished. Intervention is good, Prevention is better. It is moments like these that if one person sees domestic violence in a different light then in that moment my job is done. For that moment.

This information is for everyone. Not just someone that may be being abused.

That is one of the greatest myths out here. People who have never experienced being abused feels exempt from learning about domestic violence and sexual abuse, until it becomes personal. Until it strikes close to home.

Our sons *and* our daughters need to be taught.

About love and respect and being safe.

Neither can do better if they don't know better.

*****

Including men as victims don't always go to well. I have been asked at venues to not bring it up or asked why did I include it in my presentation. My response is always the same, *Domestic Violence does not discriminate*. That is not just some tag line for me. I can take it a step further and say that education is for everyone. Information is for everyone and in order to do my part in reducing the number of occurrences, I provide the information *for anyone* who wants it and is willing to accept it. Including men. I am non- discriminatory. As I was being victimized, so was my son. He was more than a witness to the abuse, he was being emotionally, mentally and psychologically abused the entire time that I was being abused. He endured shame, judgement and isolation just as I did, only through his own eyes as a child. I am quite sure that what he felt, saw and experienced did not hurt him less because he is my son instead of one of my daughters.

Over the years, I have had the opportunity to engage with men while consulting for an organization that provide services to men and women with legal histories.

Working with these men provided insight to the other side of domestic violence, their perspective as a victim and also as an abuser. Some of what I learned shocked me and some saddened me. The stories I heard while there are forever etched in my mind. Their stories are not only similar to my children stories but to countless other women and children. They were men with various backgrounds and from various nationalities and held a variety of beliefs.

Being in a position to interact with both abused men and offenders help me to grow into the professional that I am and it helped me to grow personally.

It made me more determined *not* to operate from a place of bias and judgment. It created in me a sense of impartiality in the sense that this information is for everyone regardless of who they are. These experiences and exposure to a group of abused persons, men more specifically, became teachable moments for me as a woman who had been abused and for whose only son had been more than just a witness to what I endured.

There was no discrimination on how the violence had impacted their lives or how they felt reliving those moments as they spoke about a time long ago yet ever so present. Some were abusers who had no qualms about speaking freely.

I wasn't there to judge. I was there to learn.

What I discovered is that many share the same concerns that women do. Most that I came in contact with were actually adults who once lived in households where there was intimate partner violence committed by either the mother or father and from both sides.

While there are those that say that women don't abuse, I beg to differ since I personally know some that do and their attitudes are the same as men who abuse.

It was a very emotionally challenging time for me.

Having to sit and listen, I mean really *listen* to what that group of men had to say and remained professional not only taught me about them, it taught me *about me* and how far I had come in my own healing.

*****

As I sat with the Program Director of the center and she flipped through my credentials, I silently laughed at the irony. Here I am negotiating a contract to provide services for mothers who need parenting class as a preventive measure to keep their children. Before my journey of wellness, I would have thought how perfect this would have been for when I was a child. Living in that house of horrors and the frequent visits from the Bureau of Child Welfare or B.C. W, as everyone called it back in the days did little to make me shudder nowadays.

"Well, Ms. Lesane, I am quite impressed by your qualifications. It is not often that I interview someone who is a certified A.C.S Visit Coach."

We finalized the details and as I rode down the elevator, the memories began to flood back and all I could do is smile.

Smile because the memories no longer had any power over me.

33

WHO KNEW

NOW I WOULD BE LYING IF I said that I planned all of this out. That I planned to write this book.

That I planned to return to school to train for the CASAC license or that I planned to go to film school to be a videographer. No, I didn't even plan to get a Masters or become part of the Executive Board for the 43rd Precinct Community Council. There were no plans to become an Education & Training Provider under New York State OASAS or attend the NYPD Citizens' Police Academy and get chosen as the Valedictorian or invited to be a member of the Citizens' Advisory Council. I didn't plan on becoming a Chaplain/Chaplain Instructor with the New York State Chaplain Task Force or a Certified Visit Coach.

I *never* planned to tell my story or share my testimony. *EVER.*

I had no clue that there was a such thing as Domestic Violence Awareness Month until seven years ago or that I would find myself standing on pulpits on Sunday mornings speaking on Domestic violence. From an abused child to advocating for abused persons. *Not planned.* I did not plan to have to defend myself against those who only saw me as a victim or those who challenged me as a Thriver…or a threat.

THRIVER: My Story To Tell

The NYSOARS ATR 3 Grant? Nope. Didn't plan to be a part of that either. Being invited to colleges and getting paid to do so was not on my radar but that's where I found myself on numerous occasions. From training Resident Aides on college campuses to lecturing at a prestigious medical college to first and second year medical students. A Press Conference with Senators Blumenthal and Gillebrand regarding domestic violence and guns at Senator Gillebrand New York City office? Rally at City Hall? Nope. It was part of The Plan just not mine. Providing clinical services? Didn't see it coming. Speaking about domestic violence at a Boxing Gym and at the beach? Never!

Being invited to Gracie Mansion for the Mentor/Mentee Event and returning to my alma Mater to lend my voice as an expert in Domestic Violence? I planned none of it.

Having the opportunity to grace the stage at New York City Police Departments' Fifteenth Annual Domestic Violence Conference at Headquarters 1 Police Plaza as Keynote Speaker wasn't planned by me either but it *was* amazing. My perfectly titled presentation, *" Not Ashamed of My Story "* was tailored made for that day.

As I stood on that stage speaking and pointing to the slide listing all of my accomplishments, I was just as amazed as those in the audience. It had been quite the journey and wasn't without controversy at times. There were some that had expectations of me that I refused to fulfill and that made things hard for me. Those people and those moments were meant to be. They taught me to respond instead of reacting. They forced me to look at how my emotions were untamed and at times, my worst enemy and ironically, also helped me stay present. Those moments compelled me to stand up for myself. In essence, they

THRIVER: My Story To Tell

strengthened me and brought me to what I consider the best audience of my career, the New York City Police Department Domestic Violence Unit and finest law enforcement officers in the Nation.

As I concluded my presentation and walked off stage to a standing ovation, it was I who was saluting them for all of the hard work and sacrifices that they make each time they respond to the next dv related job. As they stood for me, *I was standing with them* and silently praying for them all and sending them blessings and prayers for protection as they protected the least of these, those families exposed to the ugliness and the danger of domestic violence. It was in that moment, that all of my hard work had paid off and that I had come full circle.

I didn't plan to go full circle with NYPD.

And I would be privileged to stand before them again at the NYPD Training Academy.

Participating in Denim Day NYC and marching across the Brooklyn Bridge for National Sexual Assault Awareness Month in April to sitting at Gracie Mansion for the event entitled "Transforming A Rape Culture", I thought about how far I had come from being molested as a child at home, stranger raped at sixteen and sexually abused as a wife to where we, society, have come where talking about rape is now mainstream conversation. I didn't plan any of it but my past prepared me for it all.

Being nominated by the New York City Police Department Domestic Violence Unit and then recognized as a 2017 New York City Domestic Violence Advocate was not in my plans. I only wanted to be a voice for the voiceless, for those that are suffering due to intimate partner and domestic violence. I tell you the truth. I had planned none of it and I do not believe in coincidences.

THRIVER: My Story To Tell

Absolutely none of it would have been possible without the journey. None of this would have been possible without undergoing the process of healing… of finding my way through the blackness of my past that once threatened to devour my future. The process is always necessary. Hard but necessary. It produces a lot of things including opportunities that if I wasn't ready for them emotionally, they would have been lost.

At that time, I was also into my third year as Vice Chair of NOT ON MY WATCH, NYC Faith Based Coalition to Combat Human Trafficking and Domestic Violence where I facilitated the domestic violence trainings. Our Five Borough Tours were my absolute favorite. Now in its fifth year, NOMW have a beautiful office and training space in Lower Manhattan where we continue to engage and educate on human trafficking and domestic violence. And no. Didn't plan my time at NOMW either.

Who knew that Doreen from 1374 Boston Road would grow up to be a part *of all of this* because of all that she was a part of and the cards that life dealt her. *I didn't*.

Make no mistake though, it is not those moments that I count among my biggest or the most rewarding moments. It is facilitating a group for women who need support to recover from their own experiences with intimate partner violence, childhood trauma and life in general. It is in advocating for a victim, a survivor, a family. It is meeting a need and having one to one sessions. It is organizing a community event on domestic violence. It is sitting in the hot sun at a health fair interacting with the community and the children. It is being available to someone on the other end of the phone or meeting someone at a secure location. Those are the big moments.

I didn't plan any of it but I did plan to recover, to heal and to get better. Thank God, I was doing those things.

I spent eighteen months as the Recording Secretary for the Forty Third Precinct of the New York City Police Department. It was quite the experience and I met some interesting people including the DVOs who will always hold a special place in my heart, it was an unforgettable experience.

In between being there and resigning, I continued to remain focused on my *Speak Up* Against Domestic Violence Campaign. Until an unexpected health crisis arose. I immediately resigned from the Community Council Executive Board when my Mija became ill and was diagnosed with Stage Two Hodgkins Lymphoma and had to receive Chemo treatment.

Duty called. Family First. *Always*.

It was surreal like most of my life, so it didn't affect me as emotionally as it did everyone else in the family. Who Knew that one of my children would one day be diagnosed with cancer?

I also decided to take a break from the SATP, Sexual Assault Treatment Program with the North Bronx Health Network, where as a volunteer Rape Crisis Advocate. I had spent the past eight years as a volunteer responding to calls to advocate and assist survivors. Within that capacity, I had also been blessed to be able to train all of the new recruits for the program on domestic violence in the ED and to also promote the program via an interview on News12. (Didn't plan my eight years there either.)

We were given the news two days before my birthday and three days before hers. My daughter's medical crisis lasted for five months and the middle of the night trips to Memorial Sloan Kettering Urgent Care were constant and draining. Her medical crisis also had a domino effect on my household.

While I was caring for her and comforting everyone else emotionally, I went in automatic pilot mode. My journey of healing taught me to resolve problems not hold on to them. Not get caught up in them or let them get them the best of me.

And not to operate from a place of emotions.

This time was no different.

I believed that she would recover and live. That is the mindset I had from the minute I heard the news and it is the mindset I had right until she completed treatment. I prayed, gave it to God and kept it moving. More importantly, I shielded us away from any negativity, drama and those who didn't know how to be encouraging or positive. Not too many people knew. Don't do pity.

We had survived too many other things, some in this book and many not, to just roll over. *No way.* Our story of survival is just so multi-faceted and covers a multitude of life issues that there is no time to lie down, not even for cancer...we just kept it moving.

On her week for treatment, that was my life. Being her round the clock private duty nurse. That and making sure everyone else was okay by keeping our normal routine as much as possible. On the week when she had some strength, it was time for her to put on whichever wig she wanted to wear and go out outside back into life.

No time to lay down and die.

Life was still happening all around us and I chose to stay in the game of life. The strained showed on my face and yes, my outer appearance suffered. There was no time to be laughing. Praying yes. Laughing no.

On the inside I was totally depleted from seeing her with no hair. It was so weird. She was born with a head full of hair and I had not ever seen her bald. But I remained as upbeat as possible to keep my family from falling apart. It was definitely a difficult time that was made easy by the two people who continued to check on me via calls and texts.

Once she was cleared to discontinue the chemo, as soon as she was well enough to move back out, she did, and I just jumped back into the work that I love. Today, she has gained all of her weight back and then some. Her hair is also growing back in although she is still clinging to the wigs. She has moved back out of my home and has just returned to work. And me? She's ok. then I'm ok.

I chose to thrive in spite of it all.

I have also chosen not to return to the precinct. My daughters' bout with cancer changed my perception on some other things and people too.

As I was caring for her, I had time to reflect.

Once again, I was at a turning point in my life.

*****

As I sat on the Survivors Panel as one of the panelists, I decided to go in a different direction. No war stories from me. My life had shifted from that. The moderator introduced me then called me to the mic:

THRIVER: My Story To Tell

" Earlier today, someone stopped me and said that they had heard about me and came so that they could hear my story. I am not going to tell my story as some of you may have hoped. We all know what happens when a woman, a person, is being abused or has been abused. We know what the different types of abuses are. We all know of the physical and psychological abuse that occurs. We know what abuse sounds like and what it looks like. We all know the ugly and hurtful words that are spoken. Words have power and so with my time I choose to speak life. And so, my story Today is about hope. That hope that pushes a victim to see that there is life after domestic violence. That there are resources. That there is a way out, a process. I had to start believing that things would change and I had to start working on my situation so that it would change. I am here to tell you that it won't be easy getting out or staying out, But that it will be worth all the work that it takes. I had to understand the power of hope. Hope is a powerful tool. It can uplift and lighten a burden. And so, it is my hope that if there is anyone here who is or have been abused, that they find hope in their situation. That today's event was about hope. That I survived it and it is my hope that you will too.

My story Today is that because I survived domestic violence I am a not a survivor. I am a Thriver. And I hope that one day some one else can become a Thriver as well.

Thank you."

34

SUCH IS LIFE

MANY PEOPLE HAVE ASKED ME, HOW did you do it, how did you survived all that has happened and not become bitter or give up. Well, there was a time that I was bitter. Very much so. But then there is something extraordinarily simple about this thing called Life

Life happens to everyone. It's almost like being a doorknob. If you are alive and breathing, *you will get your turn.* You may not believe it, but you will. It is a mixture of it all and you never know what's behind the door of the next five minutes. Births, homelessness, unemployment, illness, abuse, promotions, graduations, incarcerations, betrayal, vacations, divorce, loneliness, joy, death.

It's incredibly unbelievable at times. It is agonizing, suspenseful, kind, dark, terrifying, lonely, peaceful, deliciously wonderful, depressing, stark, filled with hope, despair, boring, exciting, tedious, exhilarating and at times very ordinary. It can also be glorious. There are no exceptions. No one is exempt. I'm not and I have learned to be okay with that.

While it seems unfair and uncertain at times, it most certainly isn't as complicated *as I first thought it was.*

In the middle of healing and recovery and growing, life for me transformed dramatically when my perspective began to change and all that had happened became a learning experience.

What happened for me and to me is that I began to embrace life just as I embraced death. I became grateful for my life and for all of its lessons.

*****

This is what domestic violence taught *me*:

Never Be Ashamed -I am not ashamed of my story or my journey. What happened, happened and there is nothing that will ever change that. I have learned to embraced *all of who I am*, where I have been and who I have become. This applies to my children as well. They are mine and regardless of where they are in their own journey, I love them dearly and will not ever be ashamed of them. Experiencing life in all its guts and glory taught me to love life and love myself without being ashamed of the journey.

The Sun will Always Come up Tomorrow- And it will always, always shatter the darkness.

When your voice is stolen, you die- I refuse to be silence because of my beliefs. Never be afraid to *Speak Up* for yourself or the things that matter to you. Speak your Truth and let it be okay when others don't agree.

Choice – There is power in making choices. God gave me free will, then that means I am free to choose. Yes or No. It is my decision what type of day I have, what my response is to any given situation. I have learned to either take control or exercise self-control. My choice, not Life's. I no longer believe that all things out of our control.

Trust and Honor my choices- I have learned to trust the decisions that I make for my life no matter *how* they play out. I can live with the rewards of my choices and I have learned to live and grow from the consequences of my choices. I refuse to leave decisions that impact my life or my safety to anyone.

*Live life on Doreen's Terms-*To live on my terms and not allow anyone to define who I am. *I get to label me* then live that label. I say who I am, what I am. Then I get to live my truths while respecting others to live theirs.

Own up to the cards that Life dealt me- I don't do pity parties. Heck, I have survived too darn much to be whining about what happened. Besides, complaining doesn't change anything. But listen to this! I do have some fabulous stories to tell my grandsons and not only will they be entertained, they will be educated and will be able to get right back up each time life knocks then down. They will know that life is a lot of things but ultimately it is what you make it…..come whatever. For me, it is all a matter of perspective.

Be Ready and Willing- To embrace everything life brings my way, *everything.* To reach down and pull someone else up. To take risks. To stand in the gap for someone. To learn something new. To Speak Up.

Never compromise my integrity or my safety- For anyone or anything. Not even for the sake of being asked to speak about domestic violence. If I have to sugar coat or water down this message, then no thank you.

Don't wear shoes that are too small - If a situation does not fit who I am and my values, I have learned to walk away immediately. Period. There is no need to force myself where I don't belong. I don't care how nice or expensive a pair of shoes are, if they don't fit in the store, they won't fit when I get them home.

Don't Be a Victim – Not for any reason or anyone.

Stay the Course- Domestic violence taught me to stay true to who I am. Evolve but remain who I am at the core. No need to audition and every reason to be authentic. What you see is what you get. I have absolute ZERO time to be pretending to be anything or anyone for any reason.

Stay away from the Merry Go Round- Going around in circles is not for me. Put me on the Roller Coaster. The Ups and Downs and Twists and Turns and Sudden Drops and the Unexpected. Yes. I want all of the things that comes with being alive. I am alive and breathing and want ALL that Life is offering. I am not done going toe to toe with Life and is going to embrace every bit of the goodness *and the madness* that comes with it. Can't do that on the Merry Go Round. Eventually you get dizzy. I don't like how dizzy feel.

*Purpose-*The most important thing that domestic violence taught me is my purpose. Knowing my purpose and understanding my position is the answer to the question that so many often asks me. *"After all that you have been through, how can you not be bitter?"*

"Because now I know the purpose of it all. It wasn't to make me bitter. It was to make me better.

Over two hundred people sat and waited for me to speak. I opened my mouth and said, *"My name is not Doreen Lesane.*

I am Doreen Lesane and I am not a victim and have not been one for eighteen years." The funny thing about that event is two things, I did not say one word from my speech that I had written and practiced for an entire month. For some reason it began to get very warm in that room and soon I found myself saying that each and every person in that room had a responsibility to do something about domestic violence. That sitting in the venue listening to speeches and presentations didn't constitute helping victims. That if they walked out of that event the same way that they walked in and with the same mindset, that they had wasted a perfect day.

I concluded with an appeal to the community of faith leaders that attended and knew that they were not pleased that I did so.

I could tell by the looks on their faces.

I had succeeded in my mission.

I was not there to entertain.

I was there to educate and to inspire and empower.

I stood there and wrapped up my speech and the crowd arose to their feet and began clapping. I moved from the podium to leave that space but was stopped by so many of the attendees that the host had to pull me away.

As I was walking out of the room a woman came up to me and said, *"I saw your name on the program and couldn't believe it was you. We met at another event you spoke at and I think we got off on the wrong foot".*

I knew exactly who she was and remembered exactly what she had done to me.

I smiled.

"Today is a different day and I am a different person", I told her.

She smiled, hugged me then gave me her business card. *"It was great to see you again. Please don't hesitate to contact me if you need anything."*

Several of my earlier experiences in self-advocacy taught me to stand my ground and to not allow anyone, no matter who they are, to mistreat me or diminish my purpose.

I offer that to others who are healing.

The difference with how I handle it all now, is that I've learned how to handle things differently. I learned to channel my anger and frustration into becoming *more focused* on my purpose and less concerned with other people agenda.

They had theirs and I had mine.

They have theirs and I, mine.

35

THANKS

DURING THE TIME I WAS LIVING in turmoil, I was unable to see that there were people helping me the entire time. But as I began to recover from those years and as my soul began to be restored, I started to remember some other details about those same years.

Details that didn't contain pain but people.

Like Ms. Louise King from St. Mary's Recreation Center and how she would hide me and my kids from him. Right there in the center. And then there was my step mother, Eva, who I met when I was seven and who loved my children as if they were her own. And just like Mary, she never judged me or my situation. Never.

Then there was Pedro, he was from the Center as well. My kids called him Uncle Pedro and he always had a kind word. I can hear him now, *"Dee, don't worry 'bout nothing. It's going to get better. I don't have the space but you and the girls could always come stay with my family."* (he and I knew darn well that wasn't true, but at least he offered.) He always made sure they were signed up for everything and anything that was happening at the center and *every year for the past eleven years* on Thanksgiving,

Christmas, Easter and Mothers' Day he sends us a text wishing us a happy holiday. Even this year.

Then there was the principal at the school that I worked out of in Harlem. He called me into this office one day because I was found in the bathroom crying..again. His kindness and compassion toward me as a person and not just an employee really helped me to see my situation through a different set of lenses. I appreciate the intervention.

The woman in Victim Services who slipped me the envelope with the two Polaroid pictures of my battered face. It was proof.

Mrs. Santana, the guidance counselor at my son's junior high school *who never gave up* on him but worked with my son instead of writing him off,

the store manager at Furniture King, who didn't charge a delivery fee so that I would have enough money to purchase bedding for my kids new beds,

the late Geneva Stephens who always, always spoke a timely word into my heart.

the principal at the Bronx school who recognized my strengths long before I did,

the landlady who didn't take me to housing court when I was struggling to pay the rent.

The manager at the supermarket who let me get food on credit to feed my children when I had no money.

And of course, Mary.

The supervisor who didn't write me up for excessive absences because I had children in crisis that required my parental attention the same time I was required to be at work.

Then there were those that went above and beyond, who genuinely was interested in getting to know me or help me through my process.

In spite of my rough exterior. And my brashness.

And what many perceived as arrogance and pride. Those two words were far from who I was.

Then there were the few. They saw the diamond in the rough and with love and compassion polished the edges so that I would be free to shine and to soar.

They saw *me* before I saw me and *they never gave up on me.*

I am quite certain that there are others. While I felt alone, I was not and I can never thank, never repay these people enough for being there and available to my children and myself. Each played a unique role. They were there when we needed them and it is because of each one of them we survived.

And yes, those that took advantage of me and helped themselves. They helped me as well. They are those that lit a fire in the pit of my stomach. It started with me out to prove to them that what they had done would not destroy me, that I wasn't just some pathetic woman that was worthless and not deserving of their respect, that their negativity would not send me back running into my hole. This group of people had no idea that the more they tried to break me the stronger it made me. The more you judged me or gossiped about me the better I became.

You see, I had already arrived at a place in my life where there was no turning back.

I was ready.

36

THRIVER

Thriver- a person who has survived and overcome obstacles and tragedies and is living now life, flourishing and developing into a stronger person than what they were and who has learned to embrace life with all of the nuance, uncertainty and glorious mess that it is.
Doreen G. Lesane

*****

IMAGINE STROLLING THROUGH A GARDEN FILLED with beautiful flowers. Lilacs, Azaleas, Roses, Tulips and Daffodils. We look and see the beauty of them but forget that in order for them to have flourished, they had to first push through the dirt. Trials, tribulations, suffering and abuse is that dirt that we humans are potted in. It is also what we grow *through* to flourish.

It is what I grew through.

When a child is given love, they grow. When a relationship is nurtured, it grows. When a flower is cultivated, it grows. All thrive.

People who have been abused *in any sense of the word*, can't grow unless and until they are loved, nurtured and cultivated, like the flowers in a garden, they won't.

THRIVER: My Story To Tell

They sit potted in the dirt from life needing to be watered fertilized and cultivated with love, empathy, compassion, respect for who they are *right where they are,* patience, encouragement and wise counsel. Those are the very things that waters crushed souls, restores and refreshes shattered spirits. Those are the things that inspires a person to start believing again, in themselves and in life.

Those are the things that cultivates and allow hope to spring forth.

Those are the very things that watered my soul.

You won't always see the hands that are cultivating or tilling the soil but trust me when I tell you, *somewhere* there is *someone* pouring the water, pulling the weeds and tending to that garden, those flowers, *that person. nourishing that soul.*

We all have the capability to do more than survive. It is a process and that process is not pretty. However, it is worth it.

I thought that there was something wrong with me and it wasn't until I went through my process of healing that I discovered that *there is nothing wrong with me*.

It was through it all and in the process of surviving that I learned to thrive. It was the only way for me to learn *HOW* to thrive,

It was *because of* my homelessness, being a teen mom, betrayed, rejected, hungry, being abused in a relationship and all of the other stuff that happen to me that I can be compassionate to others, that I can extend grace, that I can forgive, that I can empathize and encourage.

It is because of *my trauma* and all of the drama that I have grown and learned just how strong I truly am.

It is because of it all that I have learned to embrace life with all of its glorious and cruel moments.

It is because of *my journey* and *my story that I learned* that it really isn't about what happens in my life but what I do in those moments, and after those moments. Simply put, how I respond. I have already been a survivor.

Now I am a Thriver.

You see, when you have been through the fire and came out unscathed you realize, *I realized*, that God kept me for those who are coming behind me and those who are all around me crying for help. Their pain was once my pain and their fears were once my fears. I believe that they too can learn to thrive. That *someone, somewhere* can be, will be loved, nurtured and cultivated through their process and grow through their pain.

Love, Nurture, Cultivate. Thrive. Repeat.

*****

Now if you don't believe in God, I am not trying to make you. I am just telling *my story* and my story is a about my reality and my personal experiences with intimate partner violence from my perspective as a former victim and a former survivor.

I fully and absolutely believe that it was God's grace and mercy that kept me. There is no other explanation that I am able to sit here and write this book, clothed in my right mind, able to walk without a limp (or at all!) after repeatedly being kicked, stomped on and flung into walls, that I am able to function unassisted, able to laugh, love, live!

THIS is my face without reconstructive surgery!

I can see!
The flowers blooming, and trees and the cars speeding by and the squirrels digging for food and the majestic sun rising in the sky each morning.

I can hear!
The rain beating on the windows during a summer storm, the sounds of the birds chirping in the morning, the magnificent sounds of my children voices with filled with smiles and laughter instead of pain and fear, my two precious grandsons' voices squealing in delight calling me, "Gramma", the smooth flow of Jazz.

I can feel!
The spring breeze sweeping against my face, hugs from my grandsons, the soft fur on a kitten. Dirt slipping through my fingers as I pot a plant, the warm sand between my toes.

I can taste!
The sweet flavor of strawberries and pears, the spices of ginger and jasmine swirling in a simple cup of tea...the refreshness of a cold glass of water on an equally cold day.

I can smell!
The aroma of pastry emanating from a bakery, rain approaching from the distance, dinner cooking on a lazy Sunday afternoon, smoke from a barbeque, the lavender scented lotion.

Oh, how many days I have looked in the mirror and search for the scars that the Creator of Time has not only healed but also erased. The broken jaw bones and the nose bridge healed with no visible structural defects.

*****

My children are all grown up, they are well on their way to healing and as I often hear people bragging about their son the doctor or lawyer, or their daughter the teacher or program director, I just smile and think about how blessed I am that my babies are alive *and doing better.* I think about how proud of them I am *right where they are* and what they are doing. That there is no title in the world that I need for them have other than, *Healed*. I stand there and smile because my babies have made me a happy Mom just because they are mine.

Yes, He kept me so that I can show others that *there is life after domestic violence* and so I do more than live.

I balance out life with the things that means the most: being around positive people and enjoying the things that money cannot buy.

A day at the beach with my grandson feeding the seagulls and shell hunting. Thriving.

A walk through Central Park on a crisp fall day, just because I can. Thriving.

Sitting in my window watching and listening to the raindrops. Thriving.

Making angels in the snow after a blizzard. (Yes, me). Thriving.

Reminiscing with my children about where we have been and how far we have come. Thriving.

Wearing that dress because that is the dress I want to wear. Thriving.

Having breakfast for dinner after a long day at work. Thriving.

Laughing and sometimes crying, with my girlfriends over lunch. Thriving.

Doing nothing. Thriving.

Staying in prayer to keep me sane and grounded. Thriving.

And I believe that He will keep *you*, and *you,* and yes, *you* too.

37

MS. DOREEN

I WALKED INTO THE RECEPTION AREA and signed my name on the clipboard then took a seat. There were six people ahead of me, so I sat back, pulled out my glasses and newspaper and made myself comfortable. About forty-five minutes had gone by and still four of us were sitting there. I pulled out my phone and started checking my messages. Next, I pulled out my journal and began to write.

"Miss Doreen", a voice called.
"Hi. I am Doreen Lesane," I said as I stood up and approached the woman.
She smiled and said, *"How can I help you Miss Doreen?"*
"Why do you call me Miss Doreen?, I asked.
"Well," she said with a grin on her face, *"would you prefer if I called you Mr. Doreen?"*

I couldn't help myself. I burst out laughing and so did she.

I laughed until I couldn't catch my breath.

It really was funny.

And it was good to laugh. *I mean really laugh.*

THRIVER: My Story To Tell

There you have it. THRIVER, My Story To Tell and a look into my reality as a former victim/survivor now Thriver. *I have shared with you some of my darkest moments and have kept some to myself. They are the ones that are too dark for a pen to even whisper across a piece of paper.*

Yes, I have told quite the tale about what happened to me. I spoke extensively about the who, what, where, why and when and at some points probably sounded like poor me. That is far from the case.

In order to show what people who are abused go through I chose to take it there and tell my story from the perspective of being abused, the lens of a former victim and also as an advocate who is compelled to tell the truth.

How it happened is all real. Those involved are real people. Some living others passed on from this life. The scars and the medical ailments that are now manifesting themselves post abuse are real.

What is also real is how society continues to ignore the real issues that are associated with domestic violence and sexual violence by victim blaming, how the church continues to ignore the issue, how the media reports it or mis reports and how the challenges and barriers that those being abused face are not excuses.

The barriers are just as real as the violence.

The real cost of domestic violence is the damaged lives that are left behind when there is a femicide or homicide related to the abuse.

Yes, I am standing on my soapbox. I can do that.

I survived it. I lived to tell.

Others did not.

Including the law enforcement officers that answers these calls and at times, becomes victims. Killed in the line of duty, murdered for doing their job. When this happens not only is that officer life taken from them, the lives of their families are destroyed. Their parents, siblings, spouse, children, co-workers then become unintended victims of domestic disputes and intimate partner related violence.

This is not about collateral damage.

It is about the human cost associated with this atrocity that everyone knows of.

It is the best kept worst secret *to keep*.

And it affects everyone.

I have also shared with you *What Domestic Violence Taught Me and How I learned To Live* and as this part of my story comes to an end, it is amazing to me how the grief of a little girl has come full circle to the grace of a woman. I make no apologies for who I have become, a Thriver.

Yes, I know that I can be a little brash and seemingly arrogant at times but that is only to those that wish to continue to treat me from a place in my past.

I refuse to be victimized, re victimized, controlled or abused by anyone at any time in any capacity.

I am none of the negative things ever said about me and all of the wonderful things Christ says I am.

I am blessed, strong, gentle, compassionate, and capable.

I love everyone with an Agape love *and I love me.*

I am humble yet confident.

I have found my voice and choose to speak my truth which is based on my reality. My agenda is clear: To be more in tune with those who need to be advocated for. I am more focused, more intentional about Speaking Up and *how I do so.*

I will continue to Speak Up and Speak Out Against Domestic Violence. I will not sugar coat it, water it down., beautify it, attempt to dress it up, reduce it to an event, minimize its true nature or tip toe around it. I will continue to call it out for exactly what it is. Ugly, manipulative, dangerous, murderous, fluid and very hostile. There is nothing pretty or entertaining about it. It is filled with lies and deception and fear. It has infiltrated every area of life. It is a crime.

I refuse to be silent *ever* on a matter that stole my children godmother and almost took my life.

Now as I thrive, that doesn't mean that life is perfect. It doesn't mean that I am perfect. It means that I can sit and enjoy the sunshine in my living room. For no other reason than I choose to. And it is because of my journey through abuse and *my imperfections* that I am perfectly me. And free to be me.

That enables *me* to be truthful and unabashed about myself and my imperfections. It allows me to live as I choose and not bogged down from other peoples' opinion or approval.

THRIVER: My Story To Tell

I get it!

The truth is often ugly and can seem condemning but that is not what the truth is about or what my story is about. *My story* is about freedom, using my voice and giving a voice to the abused by *Speaking Up* about Domestic Violence from the perspective of a (former) victim. It's about *my reality* of how I saw my situation, how it played out and everyone involved. It is subjective. To me.

No longer am I a victim and I no longer answer to survivor. I am not a wounded warrior. I may bear the scars but am stronger than before. I am restored and better for the battle.

It means that I must continue to *self-advocate* against those who have tried to ride rough shed over me. That's okay. God got me. And I got them …..lifted in prayer and *I will* not back down from telling the uncomfortable truth about an uncomfortable crime that has been reduced to a topic. I no longer have a spirit of fear.

It means that I am free from the chains that once held me captive to a world that steps on and steps over the least of these, the helpless and the hopeless and the abused. Freed from it all.

It means that my desire to answer to the Voice that kept me as I journeyed through the darkness and into the light of life is stronger that all the voices out here.

It means that I, Ms. Doreen, have learned to love my life and life itself, no matter what it brings and no matter where it takes me.

That I am not who others labeled me or tried to make me to be.

Ultimately, I am and have became who God said that I am. Loved, cherished, valuable, worthy, humbled by it all.

And

My past does not define me.

It created Me.

Stay Blessed and Be Safe.

THRIVER: My Story To Tell

To All Survivors

There are those who work tirelessly and have for many years in an effort to make life more bearable for those enduring abuse. Their dedication and commitment over many decades gives me the hope that the work that we do is not done in vain. We do it for you.

While many pages of my story read of betrayal, I have learned to trust again. I have learned *to be.*

You can too.

It is my hope that somewhere for someone, life is more bearable and that they, that you too are learning to live and not just survive.

It is my hope that somewhere, someone will come to know that although they may feel like they are alone, they are not.

We see you.

I see you

I believe you *and in you.*

And in and over all of the silence,

I hear you.

You are stronger than you think.

And please don't make any apologies for who you are at this moment.

Just continue to do the best that you can until you can do better.

Acknowledgments

First thanks and praises go to God. For sparing my life. For keeping me for this moment. For seeing me through the darkness. It is only by the grace of God that I am able. That I live to tell my story and to write this story, so I say Glory!!

To my four babies who are now grown I love you guys beyond words. We have had some of the most craziest experiences together but no matter what, we survived and I cannot ever thank you all for loving me and forgiving me. Thank you. I am blessed to have you all as my family. Some would say that you all are lucky that I am your mom, I said *it is I* who is fortunate that you all are my babies.

To my "BabyGurl". Thank you for fussing at me to get rest and to keep at my dream. I am deeply and forever grateful to you for being the driving force behind the power points and videos and all things that are sunshine in my living room. You are the Best of the Best.

To Shawn Blanch, my childhood friend, who believed in this book fifteen years ago, long before I ever thought about it, you knew. Thank you for believing and seeing the dream for me.

Officer Shelton, from day one, you believed in all that I do. That "Hey Dee, how's it going? I'm proud of you. Keep doing whatcha doing.", each time our paths crossed was pure encouragement. And that story you told me to tell? Here it is and Thank you.

My deepest thanks and sincere regards to the following people:

Todd Bennett, your unwavering support over the *years* as I was growing out of the darkness and into who I am, makes me proud to call you friend. Thank you for taking care of me and mentoring me when I was at my worst. From the fullness of my heart, thank you for your precious time and believing in me and my family.

Brenda Collins Harris and Alison King, you two beautiful women of God who believed in me from the very start. Believed in me to do it with no questions. Thank you, Brenda for introducing me to Alison and Alison, thank you for trusting me at the House. I admire and love you both dearly.

THANK YOU to all who "got me". The me who at times would disappear and not answer calls, texts, emails, the me who oft times had an "attitude", the me who shied away from being around a crowd, or who was having a moment. These are the people who know that some days I just have to fall back so that I can regroup, restore, rejuvenate from all…and that when I came back, they were still there. Still my friend, still loving me. It is because of all of you who understood that I am not perfect but that I am Doreen, for that I say *Thank You*. For never leaving me and always supporting me without judgement or reservation.

To anyone and everyone who supported me in any way over the years, months, weeks. Thank you always. I am grateful to know you and thankful for whatever role you played in my process.

EPILOGUE

Shoes in the bag and keys in hand, I turned once more to check my hair and as I did, the faint scar that ran across my lip and the scar tissue was a pleasant reminder that although that battle was real, *so is this warrior.*

Fighting for my life had paid off.

I am still alive and breathing and singing and dancing and thriving. I hummed a little tune, turned off the light and gently closing the door behind me all I could do was smile as I thought, "1374 Boston Road don't have anything on me."

Heading out to facilitate the training was in some ways overwhelming. Me? Doreen?! Yes, I told myself, you. *You are good enough and you have earned this.*

It has truly been nothing short of divine intervention that my life would turn this way and I have learned to delight in it and be proud of my accomplishments.

This strange thing called Life has a way of unfolding in the most beautiful and amazing way from the most gut-wrenching tragedies.

I ended that day back at home in the bathroom mirror scanning my face and touching the now faint scars that adorned it. I smiled once again because the scars only prove to me how strong I am.

And *that there really is life after domestic violence.*

Quick Tips To Show Support

Believe the person when they confide to you. Create a safe space for them by respecting that trust and confidence that they have in you. This empowers them to find and use their voice.

Remember, abused persons are already afraid, ashamed and confused. Validate their feelings. They need encouragement not judgment.

Listen to understand and not to respond. Often, abused persons are not looking for you to solve their situation, they just need an empathetic ear.

Speak Up Against Domestic Violence by becoming educated on one of the many facets of domestic violence.

Then become engaged by creating or attending community events throughout the calendar year.

Together we can make a difference.

For more information:
**NATIONAL DOMESTIC VIOLENCE HOTLINE
1 800 799 7233**

1 800 787 3224 TTY

**NATIONAL SEXUAL ASSAULT HOTLINE
1 800 656 4673**

ABOUT THE AUTHOR

Doreen G. Lesane is an avid reader and lifelong learner who enjoys nature and remains committed to educating and bringing awareness about the controversial and complex topic of domestic violence through Advocacy, Public Speaking, Training and Organizing public events. She was recognized by New York City Mayor's Office To Combat Domestic Violence as a N.Y.C 2017 Domestic Violence Advocate. Her mission is simple: *To inspire others to inspire others to Speak Up Against Domestic Violence.* She is a Mom and a Grandmom. Doreen lives in New York

Romans 5:3-4
Not only so, but we also glory in our sufferings, because we know that suffering produces perseverance; perseverance, character; and character, hope.

SILENCE KILLS
SPEAK UP AGAINST DOMESTIC VIOLENCE

ENDNOTES

1. Sir Edmund Burke, thoughts on the Cause of the Present Discontents 82-83 (1770) in: Select Works of Edmund Burke, vol.1, p.146 (Liberty Fund ed.1999). Prologue

2. Eleanor Estes; Louis Slobodkin, *The Hundred Dresses* New York, Harcourt, Brace & World 1944 pp. 10, 243

3. "fear". Merriam Webster.com 2016 https://merriam-webster.com (12 January 2016), p 18

4. Daymond John, *The Brand Within: The Power of Branding from Birth to the Boardroom* (Display of Power Publishing, Inc., 2010, p. 174, 196

5. The National Child Traumatic Stress Network, *Children and Domestic Violence* www.nctsn.org>content>children-and-domesticviolence p. (27 February 2015) pp. 40-49,109,136,140-142,183,198.205,207, 220

6. Andrea Vollans, *"Court Related Abuse and Harassment: Leaving an abuser can be harder than staying"* YWCA Vancouver 2010 www.bcwomens.ca/NRrdonlyres 8541-4398-B264-7C28CED7D208/50364/LitigationAbuseFll (4 April 2016) pp. 100-101

7. Spirit Mind Body Health-How God Designed Us faithandhealthconnection.org 2005 the connection /spirit-soul-and-body (8 July 2017) pp. 181-183, 261

www.ingramcontent.com/pod-product-compliance
Lightning Source LLC
Chambersburg PA
CBHW070554100426
42744CB00006B/278